A JOURNEY FROM CONSCIOUSNESS

SPIRITUAL INSOMNIA

STEVEN MACHAT

MCNAE, MARLIN & MACKENZIE
BOOK AND PERIODICAL PUBLISHERS
GLASGOW NEW YORK LOS ANGELES
QUEENS ROAD, GLASGOW, LANARKSHIRE G42 8DD SCOTLAND

Spiritual Insomnia Copyright © 2018 by Steven Machat All rights reserved. Printed in the United States of America and in the United Kingdom.

Except as permitted by the United States Copyright Act of 1976, no part of this publication may be reproduced, stored in a retrieval system or transmitted, in any form or by any means, electronic, mechanical, photocopying, recording, or otherwise without the prior written permission of the Author or the Publisher.

ISBN-13: 978-1-68454-103-4
ISBN-10: 1-68454-103-4

Visit us at www.m3publishers.com

Table of Contents

The Physical World	7
Forward from Nephatli de Leon	17

Part One. The physical world.

In The Beginning	25
Columba	29
Mankind	31
Consciousness. What is consciousness?	55
Plants	61
Social Contract between Mankind	75
The Story of Creation	83
Community	107
Governments	117

Part Two. The Meta-Physical Game Running our Lives

The Meta-Physical World System	139
Creation of the Western Hemisphere	
New/Old World Order	151
The Columba of the US Colonies	169
Mass Democracy	177
Mass Democracy Part Two	203
The One World Order	217
Mass Democracy Part Three The solutions	225

The Physical World

Why do we never get an answer to the questions that our heart asks about life? Where are the answers?

Where do I begin after your physical creation? Well, if you are here, you now physically exist, so you do have a beginning. Go back to your first awareness of your beginning. That time you see is when you became aware you are living in a body and need to figure out what to do. So, you copy others who are near you.

But your consciousness still has its awareness. And my friends, these questions need their answers for they will never go away.

Questions Group One:

The Questions asked by everyone at one time or another in their life:

1. Who am I?
2. Who are you?
3. What is the difference between me and you?
4. Why are we here?
5. What are we really supposed to do?
6. What is the world we live in all about?
7. After this physical life what is next for us?

The above seven questions are the elementary questions of awareness. The seven have been basic questions of mankind for all ages. Then to control your thoughts, the system you live in creates these following physical questions and schools or man-made religions give you the answers, as this is the only answer, so live with it and do the best you can.

What is the organized religion's answer? You are in essence trying out to return to God in the afterlife. Behave and you will go to God, Misbehave and you will live in the fires of hell.
If you get the wrong answer, we will hopefully get the right answer together as we continue.

Questions Group Two:

1. How do we live life?
2. What is the unit of life?
3. How many units are there in life?
    a. Individually?
    b. Family?
    c. Tribe?
    d. Local Community?
    e. Regional?
    f. National?
    g. One world order?

We can break these groups into many subgroups. Are you confused? Why? The system gives you the protection you need to carry on and live inside their mental prison of existence as your flow is cut off. You just count your days no longer. For now you are living your years.

i) What is the nation? ii) Are there supposed to be many or one? iii) what is religion? iv) who is god? v) What is the team? vi) What comes first? God or me? vii) What comes first, me or we? And the infinite question, our eighth question, is there any difference between god and me and we?

The real question is why are we not a united earth. We unite for time zones. We unite for world cup games. But we cannot unite to help sustain and build a better life for all? Why? Is it because we want everyone to be just like us? Are we not made to be what we need to be to survive the environment of the land and region in which we live? Every region is different, so why can people not be different. Why can we not unite be accepting different cultures of life?

And the final question is if we all become one, what is the new game of physical life? Or is the game over?

Group Three Questions: Creation.

1. How?
2. Where? and
3. Why?

I gave you the short answer when we began this experience.

The questions you will not hear the answers to in your fixed education system of mind control are the following:

- Who is God?
- Are we all just part of God's brain?
- Is God's brain just a big matrix? God's Matrix.

I will walk you down my thought process to help you understand my thoughts on this matter.

Questions Group Four: How do we create and enforce the system of mankind's current governments?

1. By will or by force do we enforce a system?
2. What rules were we given when we incarnate?
3. Who wrote the rules of religions?
4. What is the difference between religion and God?
5. Who created royalty?
6. Who owns the knowledge of our mankind's past?
7. Do we all own it?
8. Who owns knowledge? God or mankind?
9. What is our past? Who wrote it, or what happened to the ice below the iceberg of knowledge?

   Examples being:
   - What is Atlantis? Did it exist? If so where? What are the lessons of why Atlantis disappeared? What are the twelve tribes? Or thirteen? What is the living significance of 12 in all our ancient cultures?
   - What is the Bible? Who compiled the Bible? What was the purpose of each publisher of each new interpretation of the Bible?
   - What is evolution? What is creation? Did you ever think that maybe both exist?
   - What is spirit? Is there a non-3D world?

Questions Group Five: The System

1. What is government? Do we rule, or do we lead?
2. What is the difference between being a leader with a subjective agenda, or an objective agenda?

A quick break for you all, before we will continue this awakening to questions with more than one answer.

Again, Who am I? Why am I writing this? What is my end game?

I will share this truth in the end. I am here to help you be aware of what happens to someone like me who questions rules of order to control, as opposed to institutions to educate and prepare mankind of the joys and beauties of living a physical life here in camp heaven, not on earth, where things must die for you to survive in physical form.

1. How do we protect mankind?
2. How do we make earth safe and save earth for the future?
3. Are we the answer, or are we the problem?

Questions Group Six: The current first world systems.

1. What is capitalism? What is communism? Who bankrolls each government?
2. What is an entrepreneur?
3. What is a visionary?
4. What is spiritual awareness?
5. Why the insomnia?

Questions Group Seven:

These questions are for you to ask your families and friends, as well as your peers who judge you non-stop in this physical life. You may judge as everything we do is a judgement call. The real lesson is do not convict. Now the questions.

1. Who benefits as we go about the circle of our existence?
2. How do we protect mankind as we the current living crop are the custodians for the future?
3. Does it matter?
4. What is information?
5. What do we teach first?
6. The tree of knowledge? or,
7. The tree of Wisdom?
8. Is life both wisdom or knowledge or neither?

Questions Group Eight.

The eternal metaphysical lessons placed in sacred and made secret knowledge by the controlling system of physical and mental order.

- What are myths and what are fables??
- Example of one myth being - who is Pinocchio?
    - What is the real meaning of the story of Pinocchio?
    - Are we living a world that makes us Pinocchio?
- Are we not all God's children?
- If so, how do we become the child God created us to be? Or did God create us? Are

we not a runaway thought that figured out how to become a physical existence?

Questions Group Nine: The questions we need answered of mankind's current thought control.

A) Western Religions

Religion is a Latin word of Greek thoughts that means to bind you. To control your thoughts. Why do we have controls of strict conservative order in religions sharing the Universal God of creation? Why, why, why??

- What is a Hebrew when the thought was created?
    - Why are three religions that claim Abraham as the Grandpa at religious and at times physical war with each other?
    - Where did we as mankind fall asleep? And then awakened so divided?
    - Why did we forget who we really are?
    - Why are we here and what is the living duty for their ancestors and heirs?
    - How do we manage earth and our consciousness?

- What is government?
    - Is government really a social contract between the people? An agreement to create rules and regulations to insure the safety and health of the community the government was

created to serve or rule? An agreement to create wealth for the people living under that government so duly created and accepted as the rulers or servants of the people?
- Does each social contract creating government need to adapt with the conditions on earth? What is the 21st Century social contract?
- What is the government's role in our need to keep nature as it is, so our species does not become extinct, as many others expire each day, because of us?
- Wisdom vs. knowledge? Is their blend the answer with our current awakening towards the current game?
- Why do we believe something that contrasts nature?

B) Eastern Religions/Philosophies:

- There are many sects, aka cultures, but they have two common denominators. What are those sects? Hindu, Buddhism, Jainism, Taoism and Confucius.
- To understand your part of a bigger picture.
- But all are made for you to just accept the existing order of ownership and control.

East meets west in the land that we call Iraq and Iran today. There are two rivers there that separated our cultures of East and West. Those rivers are the Euphrates and the Tigris.

My family name is Machat.

Apparently, as told to me by Robert Thurman, the Buddhist historian in New York City, the name comes from the town that was built thousands of years ago connecting the lands. The town was called Machad. It is the origin of my name, and funnily enough, it is the path I lived producing music, learning the religious and economic thought-controlled systems of the Western World, and the cultures of what we call the Eastern world. All weapons to prevent my quest to understand the common core of mankind that would allow us to build a base and become friends.

Why? To recreate what has yet to be created: heaven here on earth, not just in the matrix of consciousness. A matrix you will soon learn about. So, my lifetime desire to grow and prosper as a consciousness, not just physical man.

Foreword

"Spiritual Insomnia" was written to *wake us up!* This is the mantra that echoes throughout the words of author Steven Machat. *Wake up!* Action is so vital that the urgency was yesterday.

The majority of us are not only physically asleep, but spiritually asleep as well – but not the author. He suffers, enjoys, endures, or simply experiences, *Spiritual Insomnia*. Machat feels that we do not care enough about our human condition. A recurring concept in Machat's book is that of a "matrix," a place or womb, where things originate. These are times for crisis-intervention and this book is a manual for such.

The author tells us that he has a boundless love for the human species – and that this love is the source of his motivation for addressing us. He comes from a background of being involved with entertainment at the hottest levels (he is the author of *Gods, Gangsters and Honor*). He made a movie in England about Poet Singer Leonard Cohen, and challenged, the one-time presidential candidate, Marco Rubio, for his senate seat in the state of Florida. Steven has lectured in over 100 countries. This is just scratching the surface for this maverick attorney, author, music / film entertainment Spiritual Insomniac.

I compare his book to several others that have been written and gotten both attention and a following: *The Lonely Crowd*, 1950, by David Riesman; *The Medium is the Massage*, 1967, by Marshall

McLuhan; and *The World is Flat*, 2005, by Thomas Friedman. All of them reflect and analyze the changing nature of society, its interaction with its institutions, its interdependence on them, and the radical changes that have occurred in commerce, communication, government, trade, and the resulting mix of good and bad that we as a species must make the best of.

The major difference between these authors and Machat is that they all look outwards, they see the world and their subjects from an observer's point of view, where it is always "others", or "other things", or "other processes" that will come to the rescue to stabilize and improve society.

Steven Machat does not flinch in 2018 to cut to the quick, to observe what is far away and to observe what is closer – and scarier. He looks inward with his "soul's," intuition, with that sixth sense humans have, to help us determine our personal and societal orientation. He does what America has never found easy to do, he becomes honestly introspective.

It is this introspection that is always missing from nearly all books and comments on the state of the nation, the state of the world, and the state of the individual. This quality and process are in *Spiritual Insomnia*. It is this inward directed examination of the multiple factors that interact in the makeup of our society that is at the heart of Machat's impassioned observations. Machat takes a wide, inclusive look at our presence, outcome and responsibilities. He moves on to examine the species from a sociological, pedagogical, historical, metaphysical, ontological and spiritual perspective!

According to Machat, we have fallen asleep at the wheel! He points out that someone (a series of criminal, societal thieves) have absconded with our thought processes! He then focuses on the "social contract" between us and those that govern us. He is a new kind of Prometheus making and stealing fire from darkness to give to humankind.

This is more than a timely book. It is what Machat calls a clarion call to action before the dream of an almost "Camelot," a potential New Atlantis, are all monsooned forever into oblivion.

Toward the end of September 2018, the president of the United States, Donald Trump, spoke to the world at the United Nations. "We reject the idea of globalism and embrace the doctrine of patriotism..." He launched a 35-minute attack on the U.N. world values of solidarity, globalization, and on respect for international institutions such as the International Court of Justice that prosecutes genocide, war crimes, and *crimes against humanity*, such as dropping bombs around the world and the kidnapping of children in America and putting them in cages. This has been done with immigrant families arriving from violence-torn countries in Central America, seeking asylum, after fleeing on foot. Already they arrive traumatized, and America wrings them through an even more inhuman trauma of breaking their safety zone net, their families, sending them to concentration camps far away from each other.

Could our problem be that very often there appears to be no *accountability* or *consequences* to those higher up, or those with an official gun, as there are for the rest of us mortals who do not belong to the top 1%, or have a powerful position in government? Machat does not quibble with words when he says that certain groups such as bankers have their losses socialized (citizens pay for their failures or planned and intended crimes) but their gains are individualized (only they enjoy their successes). Who can really accept the "too big to fail," justification? Nobody does, but this is exactly what the government force upon us.

It is therefore not surprising that a sensitive human being of today would have Spiritual Insomnia. This book is an impassioned call to action against what our Rip Van Winkle sleep has allowed to happen. Wait, he slept for only 20 years, while we have inherited a slumber longer than 200 years! The alarm clock has been ringing long enough!

Our nation's society, culture and government have suffered a break-down. This book is also very much about identity, where the loss of our perception has rendered us incoherent. We have become rudderless in a sea of troubles. If we are made in God's image, then we must act God-like and not play an unreasonable God – decide that the creation is for us to do what we will, regardless of consequences. The "history repeats itself" cliché is more than apropos here.

To paraphrase Machat, "Look at the criminals in government! Look at the criminals at the Supreme Court! " These are my words, not his. This is because we are all Steven Machat. We all must face our own *Spiritual Insomnia* and become active, watchful sentinels of our survival.

Steven Machat, the ever pro-active optimist, tells us we can do it, that we can save ourselves, and I believe him. *Spiritual Insomnia* is more than an alarm call; it is also an uplifting empowerment, a reassurance that we have what it takes to *wake up* and to bring about change for ourselves, and for our global community.

Nephtalí De León
Chicano Poet, Author, Muralist Painter

Part One.
The Physical World.

In the Beginning

Is it your beginning, or mine? Are we from the same source, or are we different creations? If so, what is the game? To win favor with the boss so we get to live with the boss? Or to do what we are capable of doing and create a world for all of us to live in and survive and thrive in the now, our present, and also so that the future visitors have a present?

Follow me as I lead you on a yellow brick road of awareness to our individual and collective life here and now.
You awoke from a dream and you are now inside a baby. You see, you hear, and you are about to learn you can taste, touch and feel physical bodies. So, where are you?

My friends, you fell into a body. The body your parents gave you by contributing their DNA as well as your mom's RNA from her matrix, the oven of life, where your consciousness swims like a mermaid into this physical land-based life.

You become aware and cry from the body you are now in, this is your Earth prison cell. An oxygen tent to allow you to explore physical life for the internal and external life you now physically have.

Your physical existence has a beginning here on earth. Your eternal existence has always existed, and this is just a trip into a new dimension for you to learn and experience the game of awareness into an endless desire to discover what you really are.

This is your dawn. You have no future fears. You look around and the world astonishes you. You can smell and taste the perfumes of life. You can see the dimensions in 3D form.

You cry, "What just happened to me?" Maybe you were spanked to make you awake. This was one trip you just had, and now you must learn what to do and how to do it while you remain a prisoner here on earth. Your parents are your first teachers. They got greedy and wanted babies. You got greedy and wanted more life. You will both serve each other in this endless pursuit of growth.

You are required to eat the creations of life. Everything here on earth is created from a gas that liquefies and materializes. Then it can go in reverse mode to alchemize a new form of earthbound creations. There are rules to live here on earth. There are desires and needs to live a full and productive life. This book I have written is to open your minds to the eternal truths of you, both you the person--- and we the consciousness we all came from.

This book is dedicated to everywhere I have touched, felt, tasted and listened to, as well as seen on my endless pursuit of mankind living in the material world.

So, my friends, open your minds and then open your eyes, this physical life will last for as long as it lasts.

Just a few words about myself before we take off on this journey.

I am a soldier of love just as you, and a missionary too - a pilgrim on a voyage to learn and share the beauties and pitfalls of this game of life.

This to me is my 65-year living testament to what I have learned, as well as remembered, all designed to share with you. For you are all my brothers and sisters, whatever your age may be. We are all God's children. We are all one race with many cultures and individual differences that make us unique and special. In fact, quite extraordinary, if we let ourselves live to thrive, not struggle for the legal tender to just survive. We must create a balanced world where love is the answer. We must help each other build our collective paradise.

Like a few of us, I do communicate with my ancestors, and God. I constantly ask my questions and in my sleep, I get answers. Which are really more questions.

I have lived many lives with one constant throughout. That constant is my quest for knowledge and wisdom. Many are raised to accumulate material wealth, learning just knowledge of how to play the current systems game of possessions before community.

I learned that game and have played it too. But it left me with a hole, a big one in my heart, as I need and want love. This heart is where love lives. The heart is God's home. And when we need God, we can feel God's hands soothing our heart. Just ask for God's love. God will answer. You do not need a third party to speak to God for you.

Columba

For every individual, whether they are passionate, a follower, disenfranchised or fugitive from the system of thought control of our current systems that are supposed to be serving us, Spiritual Insomnia takes you deep into the rabbit hole/void where you will become aware and understand how these systems are created. Learn how they are enforced as well as how these systems serve the few by owning and controlling the knowledge of mankind's existence and purpose here on earth.

You will begin to understand the function of these systems in an effort so we the people gain the strength to collectively take back our power. People collectively are the power.

This is the message and this is known forever more as the Columba.

A Columba is literally Latin for a pigeon that carries a message. We think that it must be a pigeon so we do not understand that it is the medium that gets married to an image. Then that image is what the image projects in your minds as the message that the creator of the message wants you to believe.

Columba's when created serve the purpose of hiding the reason the message was created. The message is to control the way we see our world.

My goal here and now is to have this book as the Columba for our 21st Century world. My message is love. My message is never give up. Take back your world for you and your heirs. Let's do it now.

This current system has existed ever since we, mankind, created the written word. We then create organizations that own and control your powers to create and interpret on both the meta and physical worlds of reality. The Sacred Truths are hidden inside certain words.

Our current systems are all interconnected. These systems to name a few, are your government, political parties, media providers, school systems and worlds organized religions. These systems again are interconnected and work together to do everything they can so you do not learn that you are a unique, special and extraordinary person. You are not just a number.

The word *Genius* in Latin translated to English means to be in touch with spirit. Higher spirit, I hope. For there are evil Geniuses too, like Hitler who speaks with other powers and then translate those thoughts into actions and materials for the living world of ownership and control.

My goal is to get us back to higher powers and God, so we can all enjoy the world we thought we would live in when we agreed to incarnate again here on earth.

Mankind

The game called physical life. Let's start with you. Who are you?

You start as a dream. Your parents play their sex organ instruments together as one orchestra and together, create their song, You. But now as a song, you are your human earth creation separated from their dreams to live life here on earth.

You are a living vibration of love. You acquire other instruments inside this body of yours that have their own vibrations. These instruments, which are called organs, have their own needs and desire to work in harmony to keep this machine alive for you to live and experience three-dimensional life.

But your consciousness, you the being, existed before your earth creation. You came through your parents to live life here on earth. You came to earth to live this physical earth life.

What is earth life?

It is you, and everyone else, who is in an earth 3D body sharing the air that you breathe. Drinking the water that air becomes and eating the food earth makes for us to sustain our bodies, as well as give us the energy to physically do what we do.

By the way, all your ancestors and heirs have breathed and will breathe the same air. The game of earth life ends when we change the air so our bodies cannot breathe. More on this later.

Again, I ask, who are you?

You are not a number. You are more.

You are a special unique and extraordinary individual who is a member of the group called humans.

What is a Hu-man?

A Hu-man is one who lives on earth and is able to think, create, dream and build your castles, both vocally and with physical action, in the sand that we call earth.

Why are you here? You came to earth so you could touch and feel, as well as taste and hear and see in physical forms. The physical forms you feel are fixed. Your thoughts have no boundaries BUT your living physical realities do have boundaries.

You came with spiritual awareness that you forget when you incarnated. Three-dimensional life is hard on you. For you now have boundaries to your thoughts. You must build your dreams to make them a 3D reality.

To make your thoughts, really dreams or nightmares (you choose as you are in control) become physical living 3D realities you need a team. But to have and be a real part of a team you must have health. Your body was made to flow, not get stuffed up. No doctors to stall a disease. But health to prevent disease. I call this real health.

Real Health

What is real health? One word, Balance.

Real health balances the rules of earth's life. Real heavenly health is to balance your mind and body and heart, not just your soul continuously. Plus, real health is to make sure you and our consciousness of individual parts (includes our sperm and eggs) continues after our current lifetime experience.

We need to understand that our body is really a plant as its base construction. The body then creates internal instruments that gives us the ability to do our moves. Plus, the body houses your mind and your soul, our collective consciousness and GOD.

The mind is memory and it is a tree of knowledge. It will instruct you to survive. Your heart is your green light, aka God, and it is where the wisdom of who you are resides.

And remember you are three parts. You, We and God. You the individual. We the collective consciousness where our individual identity comes from. God, where we all come from and in the end go back to. The game of life is for you the individual and we the collective to go home to God alone, without your divided parts.

What's missing in our education system is you are not taught that you have a third internal eye. One that can reach back into the matrix of all living thoughts and get back to the higher powers of thought and understanding. This I will go through later in this book. For now, let's just deal with physical life and the duty of a community of all ages to teach all of us how to survive, to thrive, not just to exist.

Today, we exist to be the slaves to those who know the sacred truths. The truths those in control make secret to keep us under their thumb.

So, to make life our Garden of Eden again we must learn how to have real, balanced health. Again, I repeat as this is a mental exercise that must be repeated so we feel it and get it, *real health* for both us and our future beings whom we live to bring here to earth.

We need to keep your plant-physical body healthy. And to do so we must honor and protect the earth that makes your body. For earth is where we feed. The food we eat, the water we drink and the air we breathe. It is a triple-header.

And we need to feed ourselves healthy earth-created foods. Today we are feeding ourselves man-made chemical copies of earth's food. That food does not have living life and to live life to its fullest we need living organisms from earth. Not the GMO's alteration from man's minds. Our organs need biology to exist and thrive. To make our earth bodies the best-balanced machines the bodies were made to be.

Earth is balanced and we, part of earth, must maintain that balance or we will lose the balance of our physical bodies if we change our nature blueprint composition. In truth we are a collective consciousness, divided into smaller parts, exploring physical life in our earth body, oxygen tanks made to breathe and feed here on earth.

Our earth body is a mother earth creation that acts as a living body suit made to house our consciousness here on earth. Mankind's body to live here on earth? Yes. How does it work as such? It is a team sport, your body. Make believe it is nine major independent team players, a baseball team of sorts, different players making one team on the field of our earth-based machine body. And we have a full-time designated hitter that makes sure we stay on the field. That hitter is our lungs.

Let's call these players organs. When balanced, those nine and the sub-team of all the parts of those nine organs, make us one great earth- made body. What are these organs? Well, here we go. Please follow me as I explain.

A. Skin

The skin is the biggest organ and its major role is to maintain the bodies' temperature. How?

Please follow this short recap of the skin.

The skin has sweat glands to cool the body down. The skin also creates goosebumps-raised hair on many of us to trap heat in the body. The skin has oil glands. Oil glands help your skin stay lubricated and keeps you from drying out. Also keeps your hair from drying up and becoming very brittle. The skin sheds cells that help keep our skin tight and effective.

Without the skin we would have no cover. The rest of our body would be exposed to the elements. We would not be us. Honor your skin. Listen to the skin. It will talk to you by making you aware the skin exists. What you feel is the skin saying to you remember me, I am uncomfortable.

I discussed above the physical truths about our skin. Here in profit-first land we have created chemical creams and chemicals to redo your face and other exposed body locations.

My worldview is do not do it. These chemicals are not made for your body and just as digging for oil or fracking our lands and seas, is no good for you and earth, so is putting lab created chemicals on your outer body. Now organic creams from flowers and plants is a different think.

But the chemicals get in your body and will change the balance of your body. It can not help you except for short term fake appearances.

This is not health care this is pure wrong behavior. Stay organic. And learn how to balance these organs by staying young at heart. And living only an organic life of no fear. Not understanding fear makes you suffer both inside and out. You wear your inner as well as outer fears.

Makes me think of Oscar Wilde and his story Dorian Gray.

B. Brain.

What is the brain? The brain is in reality the CEO of our body. Not the creator but the administrator. The brain is also in essence our living computer. It will do what our heart wants it to do or what the animal instinct of survival gets us to do. The truth is it's your choice how you use as well as run your brain.

The brain will think for you but never with higher knowledge. It reacts to your emotions and desires. Those desires are earth responses or created from higher desires. Your non-earth consciousness. Well, we live in a world of earth desires. We have lost our spiritual awareness. I will share more on this later.

The brain stores information. A living computer. Information is knowledge. Information is not wisdom. Big difference.

The physical brain allows you, the consciousness, to think -- actually to remember. It is your connection to earth and earth's physical connection to your consciousness. The body inner controller seeing eye is the third eye. It is internal, and one must learn how to use it. When you opened this eye, you are in touch with your higher spiritual power.

Wisdom at times becomes a moment-to-moment call when you review the circumstances of life. You must be fleet footed. Yes, you can make plans but remember life is a crowd game with many participants. Be prepared for the uncertain to happen. When it does, do not panic. Take a deep breath through your nose, hold your breath, count to ten, then exhale. Open your eyes and you will see that everything is ok once again. Plus, you will be in the flow and know what to do.

The brain is where the information to tell your daily vital functions to keep you moving and alive is initially internally published to be released for the rest of your body to read and act on. Those vital functions are 1) breathing, 2) blood flow in and out of the heart and 3) your digestion of elements that you put in the body. Elements to give you the energy to move and not just exist.

The brain is the communication tower of the body. When you are happy, sad, in pain or ecstasy all those nerves tell your brain, "Hey there, this is what I am feeling so tell the consciousness to be aware of this feeling".

The brain is soft tissue and is protected by the skull. Head injuries are serious. Just like dropping a computer. The system may malfunction one way or another. So, will your brain when it is hit. Direct or indirect there could be damage. The brain must be kept aware and balanced.

C. Heart

The balancer. The scales of our internal justice and the organism that makes our physical body move. The heart is the internal balancer because the heart is really the spiritual eternal and physical life is communicating with God.

The heart is our temple, church and mosque. The heart is not just a machine, like the brain. The heart is where God lives and is the true higher guide if you listen to all your thoughts before your moves. Drop the he in the word and you will see that we are the art form that God allowed us to have so we can have a physical experience called alive.

The eternal heart must control your earth-based animal impulses. In this physical machine life, the heart's job is to pump oxygenated blood throughout your body and receive deoxygenated blood back in return.

Oxygenated blood is blood filled with oxygen from the lungs. Deoxygenated blood is sent to the lungs where the lungs remove the carbon dioxide and place oxygen back in the blood. This physical role of the heart, I repeat, is that of a machine.

Balance. Life is a big game of balance. Here is our first living example. What does earth do with the carbon dioxide when we breathe it out? By breathing out, we give it to the plants that use the carbon in the air to form their tissues. This is called photosynthesis. Photosynthesis is the exact opposite chemical reaction that we create when we breathe. We need both or we will not survive. Again. A scale of balance.

Where are those plant tissues? Well just look at their roots, their stems, their leaves as well as their fruit. Those four are the tissues of a plant. The tissues are the plant skin and arms as well as legs with the flowers and the fruits. In essence the finger nails containing the glucose we need to stay alive is a fruit or is a flower the essence of the plants' love, that we smell, for we are not capable of hearing the flowers' voices, called vibrations.

Physical life on earth is one big circle, life is not a straight line. It is a circle that has its ups and downs and then begins again with a new body using the same elements as before absent your holy ghost. The invisible energy we call a ghost, we know as the essence that gives us life.

Our individual life is a time line, but our body returns to earth and will manifest again. Our consciousness returns to the eternal matrix and we then choose where we go from there. I will share more on this eternal truth later.

Now, just a quick sidebar of thoughts I must share with you. When we physically release carbon in the atmosphere from fossil fuels in our manmade machines that are not part of nature's living design, we are changing the balance of what life is made up of here on earth. If we keep doing it what will happen? We have an excess of carbon, so we must create a use for this extra carbon or not produce it.

Why? Life here will change. Too much carbon will change the balance of carbon to oxygen. Change the balance of animal and plant life. Change our seas and then where do we as a consciousness go from here? A song that we don't want to have to answer. Promise.

Back to our heart:

What happens when we oxidize our blood? Iron carries the blood through our system and feeds the cells the oxygen. When oxidized blood has an excess of iron the body does rust and again we need balance. No different than cars of old. Our bodies begin to rust. The heart is the fuel pump to live life and to balance your physical and higher consciousness needs.

The heart must be balanced. The heart must balance the spirit of life with the physical realities of this life. Fear and hate can cause your system to unbalance your heart which then makes one a beast, not the angels we can be, and remain, if we learn to balance the emotions of thought that run through our heart. And again, physically the heart does its job of getting oxygen all over our body.

D. Kidneys

Life as I just shared with you is a physical sensation, as well as an eternal dream come true. We get to live out our pre-earth birth wants and desires. For what purpose? We will get there in the end of this book.

The kidneys are located under our ribcage in our lower back. We have two. We only need one, as you can survive with just one. But you shouldn't.

The role of the kidneys in our physical life is to take the water and the salt out of our blood and produce the urine that we give back to earth. Which external urine does help earth do its thing for all other living beings. That processed human urine feeds the plants the mineral salt the plants need to grow and thrive.

The kidneys also produce renin. Renin is an enzyme that, I am told, plays a big role in regulating the blood pressure of our heart. Yet the blood pressure drugs that our corporate pharmaceuticals push on to doctors and pay scientists to say in some cases, is okay, actually harms our kidneys, which helps regulate our blood pressure.

This is putting paper profits intentionally in front of real health care. The pills we take in many cases become a band aid to temporarily stop a problem. It does not cure the cause of our disease.

The real goal of health care should be to prevent the onslaught of disease, not just fix it for as long as the medicine can. The profits before health individuals running and hiding behind the corporations' veil, know this truth but believe it will not catch up to them at this moment. When it does, they will have new cures to sell you for the damage just done.

Chemicals are not capable of curing in our life span, long term organic life. Only biology, living organisms can perpetuate life in real terms.

Follow this please. Whatever we put in our bodies must be alive at one time. It must have cells with electrons and protons as well as the neutron holding the energy of living life. Chemicals do not have living neutrons. Life and its creation is that simple. Your cells have energy of life in the neutrons. Please understand that truth. And make people honor it and stop selling you chemicals from labs.

I will come back to this as I write the 21st century government goals later but for now mark this down.
- <u>Big world-wide business today, based on corporate capitalism, is not a system of creation. It did not create anything. It perpetuates what has been created to the detriment of the public as a whole.</u>

- When those in control learn the truth of their medicines and GMOs, unfortunately, the beast takes control and says, "Screw them, as I and my family must profit no matter what." So, they continue the wrong behavior.

Now going back to the kidneys and renin, the kidney-created substances apparently is used to internally balance your blood pressure flow. When this blood pressure is out of whack so is not only your physical system but so is your ability to receive the words and thoughts that your heart produces. You can become an animal solely existing to survive physical life.

Remedies, like meditation, get your blood pressure down, more than just pills. <u>Maybe your lifestyle does not work anymore.</u> I learned this lesson more than once. Just saying.

And when your kidneys do not work, you will die from your urine poison or high blood pressure. My Grandfather Sam Golden, whom I am named after sure did.

Health Care: Sidebar, today we know GMOs (genetically modified organisms) are bad. We know as a society of consciousness that fossil fuel energy drilling and fracking must stop. We know that water must be nature clean, not purified by chemicals we dump in the water. We know the air that we breathe must remain clean free of radical chemicals from fossil fuels that we put in the air.

If you study Greek mythology, look at the fossil fuels as Titans buried by the second-tier gods of the earth. There is a reason then that the Titans had to remain in the ground. There is a reason today why this fossil fuel must not be allowed on our surface. Pure is not nature. The world is getting out of balance by man and man's abuse of earth for man alone. Our lives are in balance. Let's wake up!!!

E. Liver

The location of our liver is the upper stomach, called the abdomen. The liver is to the left of our center---stage left of the body. The main function of the liver is to produce bile. Bile, when formed, is sent to the stomach so we can digest what's in our stomach. The liver also regulates blood sugar through its use of insulin.

This truth I well know, as a type one diabetic for most of my current life. This is where our body converts sugars and stores them for our blood to use when needed. And the liver filters out toxins such as booze and pills, to a certain degree. Too much of these chemicals and the liver shuts down. A benched liver no longer actively plays your game of life, and your body loses balance and becomes toxic, and then premature death results.

This organ, the largest internal organ, is where our body gets its cholesterol. Fats are broken down in the liver to sugar. This is where diabetes two takes place. The liver cannot break down the substance abuse of GMOs as well as fried food, as well as booze, as I stated previously, as well as all substances not made by Earth in the first place.
Screw with your liver through your lifestyle and you will lose the balance of life. You will become a wounded animal first.

F. The Pancreas

A moment for a little sacred knowledge: Pancreas the word, is a Greek combination of words. Pan for all, and creas for flesh. Creas is the Latin version and in Greek it was written with a K. So, if you see a word beginning with a C and sometimes K you now should be aware that the C sometimes is the Latin version of the Greek word with a K. The name in Greek referred to edible meat.

In our current life form, the pancreas gives us creatine, which is energy. This term was used to explain the molecule found in the muscle of our skeleton that stores our energy. The energy does come from the pancreas. And what did the pharmacists use in their steroids to make us have more energy? Chemical creatine, which, my friends, will totally screw up your bodies when taken in excess.

Why is this important? It is important because our current knowledge is not new knowledge. It is remembered knowledge. We incarnate with the knowledge. Our consciousness living in the netherworld called the Matrix, is the invisible set of hands that created our bodies so consciousness can have a physical earth experience.

l must say what I truly believe here and now. We were created with the intent to be created. Our existence is not an accident. Who created us? Not God, my friends. No, we left God, the whole, and because we had separate wants and needs as first a consciousness that then splits into many parts. The same way a living cell divides we created this physical world for us to swim into at the moment of living creation. It is opening for our individual spirit, called soul to slip in during the reproduction stage of living life.

We left God, the whole. We are in essence free radicals to God. And God is waiting for us to return. We will return when we have no more wants or needs. When we agree that what's best is to live the eternal bliss of God. What some call Nirvana.

When we fall into our bodies, its traumatic, and we spend until we are between forty-fifty years of our life remembering why our individual consciousness wished to incarnate. But before physical birth, we know a lot. Our current knowledge controllers of the world erased our history in their teaching to the masses. Then teach their story not our story. But the truth is out there to discover. One must only look. And remember, naked truth will set you free when you use it as the get out of mental jail card.

Our pancreas is located behind the stomach. The pancreas produces enzymes for the stomach, insulin for the blood, and glucagon to maintain the insulin levels for the blood.

What is Insulin? Insulin is the hormone that allows our bodies to use the energy in our body-called glucose. Glucose comes from our body when we digest the earth-created products in what we digest from what we ate or drank (put in our throats to digest). It is the mechanism that makes us run in championship earthly form. Insulin, when regulated, keeps the sugar level in our blood from being too high or too low, or balanced.

G. Stomach

The stomach has a very important but easy role. The stomach receives the food from our esophagus and then sends the food on its way to organ eight, our small intestine. What this body part called stomach does for our earth body oxygen tank-suit is break the food down and mix it with the digestive juices or our internally composed enzymes.

It is part of the engine that must be balanced in order for us to operate in championship internal and external form.

H. The Small Intestine

The Small Intestine, using the enzymes (which I must now add is called chemicals by some) created by living organisms to do a biological job, to create them. Not pharmacists in white robes. What job? The job is to digest the food. The small intestine also absorbs nutrients from the digested food through a process called villi, tiny hair-like protuberances that line the stomach. Using these villi feeds the nutrients to our blood.

Using muscle contractions, the remaining skeleton of the original food, now in new forms, but useless to our bodies must be removed. How?

I. Large Intestine

The large intestine is located in our abdomen. The food is now digested and is separated as water or material that we call shit. Get it? This is where we get our waste separated and on the path to leaving our body. Once departed helps mother earth's other creations. Our waste in the human body is organic and does help the circle of life, which is nature.

The waste we make changing nature is not organic, and actually, when stored, destroys the current balance of nature. Why? Because it is not refined, so other forms of the living can use this excess and it sits, and sits, and takes up space, waiting to be digested and turned back to its original form.

Life is alchemy, my friends. All substances that make up the chemicals of life can be converted to the following substances:

- A gas from a liquid or solid
- A solid from a liquid or gas
- A liquid from a gas or a solid.

We, as a European white culture, allow others to teach us that we are a race, rediscovered, and living this truth - we industrialized and changed earth's balance for the few who run mankind alone. With industrialization of fossil fuels, we create scarcity, as opposed to creating abundance, by using untapped energy waiting to be lasered into making the world a better place for all.

Industrialization of fossil fuels harms life. Destroys nature's balance of the dead. It is not for the others who share earth with us.

Look again at our history. We create steam machines to move the dead. The industrial revolution started with steam machines. Machines made so we can convert substances to give us steam, so dead material could move on down the water path. When we convert the dead, we are making waste - earth balances take a different path.

J. Lungs

The oxygen tank that allows us to breathe in this body suit made for us to survive on earth. Protected by the two guards in our body called rib cages, this machine works to balance nature and us. It takes the oxygen that the plant world creates from their photosynthesis.

Our breaths allow us to operate the outer and inner physical body machine here on earth. We are not taught ways to breathe. We react. When we do react, we breathe through our mouth. We put oxygen in our lungs.

But that is not the way we must always breathe. When a baby begins, the baby uses its nose to breathe in. At the same time the baby takes this breathe in, the baby's stomach will expand. Then when the baby breathes out, the baby pumps its stomach in. Why? This circulates the breath throughout the body, not just the lungs. Our whole system of organs needs oxygen to breathe and operate so we can live in the world, and the internal world of higher power. The three-dimensional world is actually outside the matrix of creation and eternal existence. We left the matrix of creation to have external existence. This is the outer world.

Reproductive System(s).

How do we continue mankind into the future? Well, we reproduce.

How? We have what we call sex. And to have sex we have some form of romance to get our sexual organs going.

Man, and Man with a womb. The two halves of Hu-Man consciousness that in the end does what every living organism does. We reproduce.

When we reproduce, we create a new physical being just like us. Made from our combined DNA. DNA being the blueprint of our bodies. The DNA tells the new living organism the body suit it must build for us. This DNA chooses if our body will have a womb or not.

I believe we choose our parents and we choose our sex. We do not get it right all the time. I believe some of us come to live to have a female or male experience and end up in the wrong body suit. More on this later. Right now, I will just focus on the physical creation.

How do we reproduce? Our body combines in a play where we use our organs to release the energies stored inside us that will create a human being.

The male body has sperm. The sperm is stored inside the male reproductive organ called the testis. Until fully developed, the sperm is located in the back of this organ in an area called the epididymis.

The trick in our lives is to avoid temptation to live a reckless lifestyle. It will hurt both you and your potential future. Know what you are doing. Know your body. That is why this section is the lead off to the answers of my spiritual insomnia.

This is from a Cuban website with no name attached that I am reading while I am here in the Keys of Cuba, June 25, 2018. The day my son was earth born again.

> *"A healthy sex life is a very important part of life for most men. Men's reproductive health is dependent on the health and proper functioning of the external genitals, internal sex organs, sperm, semen, and male sex hormones. Men's sexual health also includes fertility. You may assume that women are mostly responsible for infertility, but men's health issues account for half of all infertility cases. Protect your sexual health and fertility by living a healthy lifestyle and avoiding risky behaviors. If you notice pain in your groin area, have problems maintaining or getting an erection, or have problems with ejaculation, you may need to talk to your doctor".*

Now how do we reproduce scientifically? We man without a womb have our penis play inside the woman's vagina which will be wet with the emotion of desire and hot to cook our penis in a sea of personal ecstasy to get us to release our sperm in this dance between the two sexes. The end game is that the sperm will catch the egg coming out of the woman's ovary into her vagina.

The vagina is the opening to the world of the womb. It is where we fertilize the future in this act, we call sex. Which is heat-generated so the sperm and the egg released from the ovary combines with the sperm and the explosion of new life.

Life begins in my mind when the individual consciousness, which I call soul, enters the body and becomes the living spirit of this new body suit. Takes nine earth months to build the suit most times. It takes maybe 16 earth years to understand how to use your new body suit.

Other animals do not have a personal ego like we do. Meaning that instinct knows how to just survive without asking the questions who what or why.

It takes eternity to understand why you choose to do this. And it takes a lifetime to learn how we must live together so all mankind and other beings get to enjoy this place in space we call earth.

In summation, please understand we must learn from and understand our bodies. This is only an opening for you to explore more all the thoughts you get inside your mind. Thoughts from beyond our bodies as well as from your brain. Listen, your body talks to you.

Funny how we buy computers (external brains) and get a handbook. But we are not given a handbook on how to keep our body machine in tip-top shape. Instead we are sold "snake oils" by circus clowns called businessmen with the intent to profit off our dreams of immortality, and more.

We need to honor our body, that is our place of soul worship. I have learned this truth living my rolling stone lifestyle of my life. I collected no living moss. Only a wealth of experience of man's many wants and needs. And I must add - meet God.

We have just discussed the body of mankind. Two roles. First is dual, to help you live and for our species to continue to live in this costume with others. The second role is to allow plants the opportunity to be our partners in this experience called life.

Life must give and take. Remember, life has both roles, or you have no life. You have a machine that will stop working.

Consciousness: What is consciousness?

It is awareness. It is the group of thoughts and collective desires as well as needs, of which we are a member. It is where we began and where we go back to after our earth body stops working as a unit. A unit that allows us to live here on earth.

We discussed the body; now let's do a brief overview of exactly what consciousness is. And yes, it survives earth's death.

Where do you go from here? You go back to consciousness. You either accept to rejoin God, or you still have issues that you will sort out in the lower matrix as an individual until you get it right.

Yes, the matrix of eternity has a system of levels. I go into this in my book *Sacred Knowledge, A Rock n Roller's Guide to Higher Consciousness.*

To get out of the levels, you must graduate by having no needs and desires. Only the eternal and unrequited love of God for all eternity and more. Remember, we mark time as our physical bodies do not live forever.

You get it right and move up the ladder, when you discover all consciousness needs and desires are to learn that the one love is God. God awaits your return.

Easy to say, but can you let go now? Did you let go before, in your last life? Will you let go this time? That is the eternal decision.

We are physical species that we called Hu-Man. Human, again, a common consciousness that landed on earth. Or better stated, fell into oxygen tanks that are really earth bodies. These bodies are like a 'car' with computer machines moving our parts (brain) and built in to the beyond with our own private frequency-radio (third eye) machine.

All the fuel to keep our earth machine going is here on earth. Our bodies were made to be biodegradable and live here where earth allows us to play with all its living creations, as long as we allow others to do the same by not destroying the balance of earth.

Earth is one big balanced pantry. Nature's limited warranty on the body, in giving our consciousness physical life, is about 108 years. It is limited because it requires us to participate in the care of the body. Maybe, if you were really lucky with the elements you cannot control, with a max of 120 years.

When we leave our bodies, the earth made parts, now separate from our consciousness, remain and decompose. Our earth parts are twenty elements. The separation allows our twenty earth created elements to be used again. Everything we physically are stays here. We cannot take it with us. But we can come back to it, when we learn the tricks of incarnation.

Those twenty metallic and non-metallic elements are the following: Oxygen, Hydrogen, Carbon, Nitrogen, Phosphorus, Sulfur, Calcium, Iron, Iodine, Sodium, Potassium, Magnesium, Copper, Cobalt, Fluorine, Selenium, Manganese, Molybdenum, Nickel and Chromium. The 21st element is the home of all twenty - Mother Earth.

When we take our last breath, our consciousness leaves this dimension, and takes its seat in the coliseum of astral world souls. Individual souls looking to rejoin consciousness in the sacred space of the matrix of existence on its way to actually first rejoin collective consciousness. We lose our individual EGO. From this point, the final ladder is the ladder home. Home is back with God.

As individual souls inside this matrix of creation we can chose to keep our EGO. Not let it go. We can choose to incarnate again in a physical dimension, somewhere over the rainbow of eternal life.

In the lower eternal matrix dimension, we wander around looking and creating a place to come back into and build our physical dreams. What I call castles in the sand that we call earth, but is really one of the physical heaven's dimensions created for confused runaway souls to live a physical life. Really, it's a life without God in what becomes people bumper cars trying to figure out how to get peace and live life, eternally.

In this eternal matrix dimension, we dream, but also reflect on what went wrong in our last life. You will meet your earth past and will connect with your earth future. You see, our astral dreams have no boundaries. We have individual needs and desires as a soul. And our dreams are directed and produced by each of us as a separate entity. Only when we realize that a soul must lose its ego, stop Edging God Out, then, and only then, we will enter the higher court of eternal life and begin the conscious effort to return to God.

We are not separate, and that is what life here on earth is meant to allow us to learn on our path, called the yellow brick road. We need a team to live a dream and this team must align with the virtues of God. The road is really the light back to God. God is everything. But God is also eternal, and as I said, God lives in our hearts. We are off to see the wizard.

Individual Life is two elements. One is earth-based physical; the other is your individual characteristics, making up your soul. It is us, as a now individual, special unique and extraordinary Hu-Man beings. What is our soul made up of?

These seven creations, really super powers, are what your soul is all about. The life energy that makes us special and unique, but apart from God. The issue is, how do we use these super powers in the game of life.

1. Intelligence. We all have it. Question is how do we use it.
2. EGO. Did we edge God out? Thinking only about ourselves?
3. Feeling: We feel. But we feel what?
4. Mind. Where we learn to be aware of our communication senses. How do we use this power? For who, and why?
5. Knowledge: What do we do with what we learn? And when do we stop learning?
6. Action: this is the game of creation; how do we make thoughts into physical reality?
7. Life-force. This is where we use the ability to create and give energy and life to our needs and desires. God created us to create. We live

love till we create fear and hate. We have free will to do as we want. We create this current living hell, changing love to fear and hate. Putting out the light to god with the twin peaks of darkness. The two, fear and hate are the cancers of physical life.

So now we have our physical bodies. Our individual souls. Our consciousness. And God. But we do have partners here on earth. So, lets meet our other half. The Plant world.

Plants

When we, mankind, see an animal or a plant, we look at them as objects. In our minds we are the subjects. So, we consider ourselves the bosses. We are not.

Lessons we must not only learn but accept and live as truth. Why? Because we must balance life but our wants and needs on a much higher level then only short-term physical survival.

The other earth animals and the plants may actually see us as an object. Their collective minds work like ours. Their question is how do I get this creature to help me better my life here on earth. How do I live better and reproduce more of myself? The question we really need to ask is How do we all coexist together? Not just how do I get more.

Yes, you read me right. For these other living beings have a consciousness based on physical survival. That survival means the here and now, and really hear this, plus tomorrow, with future beings just like them.

Dogs learned to love man. Why? We feed them and house them. We love them, and they become our four-legged babies. But as much as they love us, they love to be fed. So, they get cute and beautiful and induce us to keep them in comfort.

Cows feed us. Cows clothe us. As do other animal species. Because they do, we keep them alive as a group. Domesticated animals choose us as much as we choose them. That is why we domesticated those and not others.

It is duality. Subject and object. Other animals not domesticated, let's call them the animals of the wilderness--- choose other living beings to build their world. When we come and destroy the wilderness, we destroy so many other earth worlds. But we do not care. This attitude, mindset and lifestyle is dangerous. We must learn, believe, and live understanding that soon earth will take away the substances that make our bodies work. We need to wake up.

We do what we need to in order to have our minds and spirits controlled. We like sleep without consciousness. We do not understand there is more than just our physical world. Every time we get near this truth some organization, be it religion, or "man-made royalty" controlling our currency of mind body and soul, takes control of our minds. With this control of our minds, using fear or greed, those in control of our minds makes us live in physical fear and stop our awareness of understanding just how we must live.

We are all just like dogs, except we can feed ourselves, and we can make a government where we all take care of each other. But we submit. So, what do we do to change this man-made paradigm?

I will share my visions at the end of this tome. Just stay with me.

Let's take you through the consciousness of plants. Whose souls, for the most part, are united with their consciousness as one unit? There are runaway plants as there are runaway animals. Runaway is where one acts for their own good, not the good of the group. Humans are a runaway species. We are a cancer to earth's natural balance. And that is our crime, because we know better.

How do plants survive? One way is simple. We, mankind, and other animals in the animal kingdom help them do so. We choose them. That simple. But how do we choose them?

Way two, is that plants do learn their own survival skills. They have a consciousness. And plants choose us too. How? Well, read this and then take a moment and close your eyes and ask yourselves is this true?

Ask yourselves is this really what living things do? Make teams to survive. How?

The answer my friend is blowing in the wind, and you have just seen the wind of truth. Follow me please

What is a plant?

Creation is what our consciousness does. Bodies are what we choose to live physically in. Before our animal bodies, our consciousness, which comes from God, the one God of all creation, created building block chemicals. These building block chemicals created material substances. This is sacred geometry. Building physical bodies so we can put our consciousness into that physical machine.

Consciousness, when it left God, created the first machine of energy. That energy is the five-pointed stars of the Universe. The star is called the sun of its Universe.

And guess what, we animals who stand on our legs and have two hands, with a head, are a replica of the stars five points. That is why it is said we were created in God's image. The energy star that runs the universe you live in is called the son of God.

The sun god, which we call the sun, gave the energy to bring the building blocks, that we call cells, the energy to bring life to the machines that these cells were creating to life. That simple.

Yes, we are living one huge dream. We were designed with intent; as long as we create the big bang theory of endless creation, life will continue. So, will real evolution, as we protect the vehicle that houses creation, our living body suits, and make it work better that we live in. The question facing mankind is while we recreate ourselves, will we destroy the organic substances so related that allow us to live and dream a physical experience.

There is that invisible hand that creates, and this hand as two choices:

1. Keep using the balance of things to make us the top physical dog of earth better by taking and not maintaining or preserving what gave us the physical bodies we inhabit in this life experience.

2. Maintain the balance and keep this game alive. We cannot do both and we as a consciousness need to figure out what earth is to remain. We will destroy it real soon for our bodies to carry on.

We get their messages and we act out what role we play. Do we do as other animals do, and protect only our habitat? Or do we do what we came to life to do? That being the higher game. That game being to keep this earth the heaven for all that it can be. Balance is the answer.

Plants are so important. And as I like to say, they are so, so necessary. But we choose to not understand that truth. Plants create the abundance of oxygen that allows our bodies to play, and our bodies create the abundance of carbon that allows the plants to do their thing.

And plants have a consciousness too. They really do. We are listening to the unheard vibrations of the plant's collective thoughts. Plants are objects and they manipulate us the same way we manipulate them. We manipulate to exist and multiply. So do plants.

Plants have at least four techniques, I have learned, to get us to spread them. All four deal with playing our wants and needs like strings. The plants energy plucks our strings, and we do as we were emotionally told. We multiply that particular plant species.

How, you ask?

How does man use plants to make mankind better? It feeds us. They show us God's beauty. It also intoxicates us. Plants control us. Like a woman can, and do, control us men.

A plant has taste. A plant has smell. A plant can intoxicate us as well as create the awareness to discover the organic chemicals that make up the plant and flower. The issue we really do not wish to understand is that these chemicals have a life-force. Our attempts to duplicate them must get a life force inside the compounds for it to really work on us. The life force is what we need. Let's define those chemicals as organic, made from, and by living beings (for clarification, organic is made by nature). Not chemicals, which cannot receive and house a life force, or as the Catholic Church says, the Holy Spirit.

Without the life force, I do not care what any corporate-bought scientist or expert tells you; the use of those chemicals will not be digested by your body during your life line. And will cause harm in your body as you continue to grow and live the seasons; your body was created to have life force from birth, to earth-death.

If you are near the end, which we call death, ok, take what you need to ease your pain. But saying that plants have the same cures pharmacies are selling you - if not, what are you allowing society to do to you? Shut you down and make you conform, is the truth.

Plants, too, must protect themselves in life's balanced jungle of other beings. The plant produces chemical potions that will kill us. A plant that we feed off such as a potato, or one that we smoke to "relax," like tobacco can kill us. And a plant has beauty that we need to decorate our own indoor or outdoor world. Plants got us to domesticate them. Just like animals did. We think it is about us not seeing, while it is also about them.

One of the first stock market banker's scams of the "modern European Imperialistic world era," was the Tulip bulb explosion of the late 1500's and early 1600's in what today we call the Netherlands. Then it was still part of Spain and a member of the Holy Roman Empire of self-anointed local rulers of the local society.

People were betting through an "organized banker's form stock market" on futures. The future was what color tulip they would get from the seeds they were buying from the organized distributor of this roulette game. A forerunner to today's future stock market.

The winner was the one whose seeds became a black tulip. The seeds were not predetermined, to our best knowledge, it was potluck. The dealer's man got their money and got their distribution fee. Their own stupidity fleeced the people. Never bet what you cannot afford to lose. Always bet on yourself, know that, and follow through.

Let's move to Cannabis; let's examine the newest US craze. What is the new craze for this flower? Is it for health, to allow real wealth, or for wealth of the few to reproduce by making the plant a chemical experiment on our bodies? Capitalism vs. mankind.

So, Cannabis, aka pot/marijuana, has two potential uses. One purpose is to help our nervous system relax. Purpose two is to intoxicate our minds with the mind of the plant and make us unproductive for the capital world of work, work and more work. In the mind of the plant we invite the plant's consciousness to join our individual soul and become again a part of collective, not individual nature.

In a capitalistic controlling world, we allow drugs that alter our awareness in society as long as the drug does not stop us from working for others. If the drug allows you to see truths about yourself, the "powers that be" want that use prohibited -- It is THAT SIMPLE. I am not saying it is right - only saying what is. You are not productive to our controlling society of consumerism and debt while high on Cannabis. Unless society sells you the Cannabis and controls the growth of the flower.

So, let's go to the drugs like alcohol, which changes your disposition, and may make you lose physical control. But you can sleep it off and go to work for others the next day. Plus, you do not balance your nature, you purely edge God out. Why? Because you are not a team player, life is all about you.

This needs to change. We need to educate all on what substances affect our balance of mind body and soul. Out of balance, we change, and become animals on a hunt of fears and a path of death, all to save our unbalanced behavior.

We must learn to use earth to make our lives better, and that means keep earth alive, to thrive with the balance of chemicals that make up earth. I will get back to this, but for the moment, I feel like waxing your minds with the true beauty I have learned; that plants have a song they give each of us of higher consciousness, which call spirits and show us things. Why? Because we are open to receive the teaching. Here is so much of what I have seen on my journeys that point back to the matrix of consciousness.

A good way to understand this matrix of consciousness is to see it as a beehive. Inside these beehives is all the knowledge of mankind, plus a lot more. There are elders we can call upon to help guide us through this knowledge with awareness I call wisdom. We can get to this beehive by using our antennae, just as bees do, when they enter their beehive to gain the knowledge of what they are to do and where they are to go.

Our eternal antennae are behind our third eye. It is where the pineal gland lies. The gland that produces melatonin. A hormone that affects the modulation of waking moments and our sleeping time. A time to be and a time to become. The gland also moderates our seasonal-earth's rotation patterns for us to adjust and survive the new beginning and the end of the last season.

Yes, I believe bees do this in physical life. And I do believe that we do this in our current life using our tools around this eternal third eye.

I see plants as living paintings made by God. The plants sing to us. The plants send out vibrations that birds, bees and insects, as well as other lives can hear.

We see the plants. We can smell the perfume from the plants. We can taste their gifts they produce called fruits. We can hear the vibrations when we learn to listen to the wind. We can own them and their flowers for a while. Or we can just admire the paintings that they are.

We can watch dew drip from their leaves. We can capture this dew which some do in today's Yemen or Egypt and call it frankincense. This captured dew was one of the three gifts, we are told, that was brought to Jesus, on his birth, by the three kings. The other gifts, myrrh from a plant, and gold-stored energy from earth millions of years ago.

We surely know what gold can do, as it glitters and intoxicates many a fool. Study King Midas, who had the golden touch. Midas had to beg to be released from the wish that Zeus granted him to survive again on earth. You cannot survive on gold. It may say hey look at me!!! But gold has no vibrations except the glitter that makes many a human sell his soul to own the metal.

Watch out for the power of Gold. We sell our souls for the dreams we are told that exist by owning gold.

Why Gold?

Gold can be melted. The Hebrews did this in the second temple. Gold vaporizes as a gas and then becomes a liquid that hardens and becomes a white powder-like substance called manna in the bible. The manna was said, in the sacred schools of old, to open one's third eye. Frankincense was said to help the third eye see when you went there in some form of meditation. Myrrh was used mystically, using the plant's energy to heal your earth wounds. It was applied to Jesus when they took him off the cross--- alive, I must add. But that story is not to be told here and now. Later, my friends, or search in or on the Internet, or find it in a library.

In public, the Vatican teaches that these mystical powers do not exist. But in reality, they definitely believe in these powers. It is their secret knowledge.

Feel me, see me, smell me and taste me. The thoughts that plants send our way, in essence, by telepathy.

Plants also warn you away. How? Plants with its thorns warn us not to touch but just admire. For those plants are not for our internal bodies and our organs to consume by tasting or touching or even smelling.

Plants, like a song, trigger our memories of other times. They may remind you of that first kiss. The time you awoke and saw the lips that you had to kiss. Looking for love to unfold.

Plants may remind you of the last time you had that kiss. Plants will remind you, through smell and taste, of times gone by. They will not remind you of times to come, as those times have not been created. But a plant can get you to dream.

There is no destiny. Life is a play we live and write when we remember. To live life, which is a present, you must live in the moment.

To me, mankind is the plants and the bees. A woman is a man with a womb. Man alone would not survive; that is, until we are all test tube children. A test tube baby, grown outside the womb is not mankind. Living without organic existence. In reality, a machine brought to earth with a memory, but none of the seven characteristics of mankind dedicated to creating and learning love and hate. Test tube is without love. I believe you need the physical connection of the womb getting the sperm from the man, at the moment the magic gives you that spark of life.

The spark of life happens, and the sperm and egg combine to give life to another soul to enjoy life here on earth. The womb is really the three-dimensional connection to the invisible matrix of existence. This moment of birth is created when the spark burns the invisible matrix of existence an empty space, so the soul can be reborn again.

Welcome back.

Now a woman, just like a plant, will seduce us men to fall in love with them. They do so with beauty. They do so by creating desire. They do so with bearing fruits that attract our attention, called jewelry. They do so with their makeup and clothing all done to attract the male, so this species can continue. The egg of life, mankind's life, is stored in the woman's body. When it is set in motion to come down the aisle of future mankind, at the right time of the month, is when the woman's scent is the strongest. The woman is asking the male in her life: Pay attention to me, and love me, do as we can to make our song together, right now, with physical experience of love, and unfortunately, sometimes just the intent of sex.

I said earlier how non-human plants control us. Well, they do by becoming predictable living forms of food we eat to keep our bodies moving. Our bodies, producing the energy and waste, both we need, and then earth gets from our living machines and moving forward.

But our capitalistic corporate world of rents and consumption for this material world requires predictability and stability. Not food for our growth and development. Note; our world requires a guarantee of food supply in our urban jungle, not nature's lands of paradise.

We allow our few who somehow run and control our system of rules and order to create genetically modified organisms (GMO), aka, foods, so the output of food is predictable. A business for paper profits, as opposed to the profit of communities' life. And with knowledge by those few, not really what God wanted us to eat. Laced with laboratory-created chemicals that change the natural organic rhythms and rhymes of our body balance makes us not what we are supposed to be. BUT, it does make us predictable and dependable on the perpetuation of the drug that our food has now become here in America and around the world.

To keep the farm output consistent, which nature is not about, we change the seeds by physical man's hand, not God, to not allow non- organic food substitutes to survive in spite of not having the ability to reproduce from its seeds or its natural pollen.

Our food is also being made with chemicals called pesticides to stop pests, which balance our earth. So, this new food is sold to us without any real thought to what happens to our bodies over a lifetime, not just one year. We change the balance that nature took its entire existence to this point now, to create for us to live in the body we are.

If the game plan of the higher consciousness is to use us, like it did beavers, when their tails made dams and changed the local waterfall, then get ready for a different world and a different mankind. For we are killing our physical balanced existence.

We, as a race, need to figure out our purpose. Is it to change the world that we live in, and if so, for who? Or is it to keep the world as it is for our heirs to enjoy and play in. This comes down to our social contract between ourselves on how we are to all live on earth.

This comes down to what we call Government. And my friends, now that I walked you through the background of mankind and earth, I will now turn to answer the questions raised in the beginning. Who are we and what are we doing here? Again, it comes down to the social contract between us.

Social Contract between Mankind.

The community consciousness.

Community?

We were created to socialize. We are each an individual island that must combine socially in order to survive earth life. To socialize, we must have a moral, just consciousness that creates rules and regulations that adapt with the climate and provide equality and equitable rules for all living beings. Not just rules and regulations to perpetuate the existence of the few who somehow created the world they now wish to keep alive. To keep their system going in spite of our learning and knowledge that grows and can continue to evolve to make the world better for all.

The British tried to do this with their common law system. That system was for common man. They also had courts for royalty. Rules for royalty and their church. Privileged people.

That system was tossed when the printing press took over and people were able to mass educate and create laws to perpetuate the living system of those in control of property and your necessities to live life here on earth.

Law: Two sides to this word. Equity is for the people. Statutory law is for the property owners first. That simple.

Rules and regulations are combined in what I call governments. We need a Government of the one tribe called mankind. And we need a government representing the many tribes that man creates in geographical regions to live there on earth. Each tribe is really nothing more than a team to play the game of life with and for in the era the tribe was created.

The team is nothing but a part of the league of life. A league of mankind that each tribal team must put first if the league is to survive.

What is the purpose of any form of government?

Well, it is simply the social order the people agree to live under to provide each other health, wealth and safety.

We in the US have two stated intentions. One is our Declaration of Independence. The second is our current 1789 Constitution of law and order here in the US. The difference? We must give each other life and liberty as stated; but do we protect people's property first or to give each and every member who contributes and joins our societies the opportunity to pursue their dreams when they are ready?

This is where capitalism, which perpetuates interest-charging, rent-collecting behavior, differs from entrepreneurs in touch with God and nature. The entrepreneurs being visionaries who help make life better for all by creating a real living social order. Not one of capitalistic vampires feeding and living off of their zombies who wait to fight for the crumbs the vamps leave them. Capitalism requires you to accumulate what is, which means you must dispose those who have it now. Capitalism is a system of scarcity, not abundance. Life is abundance. Purgatory is scarcity.

We here in the US have a Food and Drug governmental agency. This agency is in charge of the food we eat and the drugs we are permitted to be prescribed. Prescribed to grow and thrive or just survive? Big difference. And where do these administrators come from? They come from the schools owned and controlled by the top line renter's division of private third-party bankers who wish only to perpetuate their fiefdom. Or the corporations who need their new snake oil approved without proving it does no harm to earth. No, we have to prove without a test of time that it is wrong.

What does this mean? Schools that teach you this is the only way. Their way. So wrong. They actually own the distribution of people knowledge, called our school system, and if someone comes out of nowhere, like Facebook, the banking system will induce you to join so they can buy your essence. Make you part of their system. But they cannot buy me. This is my life lessons, which as an explorer of the world and all people, I now share with you

Case in point. As I stated in this last section, how do we perpetuate our species? It is by having a healthy egg inside the man with a healthy womb, that we call women, and having a healthy sperm that fertilizes the healthy egg.

By changing the balance of earth, we change the reproductive organs and the eggs and sperm those organs produce to perpetuate our species. No one pays attention to this detail.

There is nothing wrong with experimentation to make life better. But there is nothing but evil when we learn that what we created hurts our species, as well as other living creatures, and with this knowledge, we hide the truth, because it would change the wealth of our controllers.

One case of many I will now discuss. Male and sperm. When we make physical love between a male and female, the male releases sperm which swims to its dreamed land called the female's egg. Millions of would-be humans swim and only one wins. You won. So, stop being the victim and let's play the game of life as a team, and end this control of the few who convinced you they are better then you.

To incarnate, you need to swim fast and know where you are going. You won that race to be you now. This truth is changing as our environment has changed. The question is; does each sperm have a consciousness? Is this where we hide before we reincarnate in full body form? Or do we incarnate at the moment the fireworks hit, when sperm and egg combine as one. This magic moment. I choose the latter.

Sperm has one head and one tail. A tadpole, if you like, to visualize. Today, many males are making sperm with two heads or two tails. Scientists, a term we use loosely, know this, and so must you. Many, and I will say not all, work and repeat what will get them paid. As will the media repeat only what their advertisers wish others to know. To know, to seduce you to buy products for their individual gain, on the most part.

This sperm and egg are changing man-made genetically - chemicals are now engineered, which is causing deformity in our evolution. That is, before we get to the fact that many males have less sperm today then yesterday's males. This is a huge cost to our social contract of living here on earth. To the quality as well as the economic currency consequences. Economics currencies being defined as what makes us move, as opposed to existing.

What is causing this sperm change as well as egg change? There is a common culprit in human as well as animal studies - if you look, you will see. The culprit is a laboratory chemical that our scientists call endocrine disruptors.

What is an endocrine disruptor? They are chemicals that can interfere with hormone systems at certain dosages. These disruptions can cause tumors, birth defects, and other development disorders, which I will get to in a minute.

How are these chemicals created? Well, they are created when mankind makes plastics. They are created when we make cosmetics, furniture and pesticides. Pesticides that end up in all the food we eat, it being animal-vegetable, or fruit or seed. Truth.

The new hormone, of man-made evolution, changes our body's DNA map, as well as the womb's RNA. This new map can cause in those who live a new outlook on life. One as simple as not knowing what your real sex is. And in the newborn, these endocrine disrupting chemicals mimic hormones and confuse the process where the mind does not marry the body, and a male physical body may inherit a feminine mind, and vice versa.

The following is what spirit has made me understand. When our individual consciousness decides to fall into a body again and have a physical life experience, we choose where we begin this new trip. We choose our parents, we choose our location. When we choose, we already know we want a feminine or male experience. When we choose the egg, believing one thing from our past lives, as we get our body suits, these new man-made chemicals change the egg, and it is too late for us. We now have to live with this new physical creation, the wrong body suit of life here on earth.

Please know this truth, no matter what religion your parent's existence at the time of birth labeled you - we were not born in sin. We were born to work out our needs and desires. Why we can not just be. We fell into our bodies to discover life and, like our declaration of independence, to pursue happiness.

We need a social order of people working together to build a land that lives with the one God. That God we Hebrews choose to follow. The God of our creation. The God of all three Middle Eastern religions. Not the man-made religions that say God chose us – therefore, we will make laws for our society. So now that God is dead, we will make you do what we thought God wanted you to do.

God is alive, and we are God's children - to build a world-honoring God, not asking for forgiveness as we kill and destroy this heaven God gave us. We were born free, as the song goes. We have free will.

There is no written pre-destiny. This is God's personal movie to see what we do when we are freed from God's unconditional love.

And know this truth. We were not given permission to kill and or maim. No, we were not. And as if we were, we need another game to play.

The 21st Century Social Contract between God and mankind: All governments must live with the present, and not be dictators of the past world. We must adapt, and so I will now give you the government of today's world. But first answer this question.

What is a government?

Easy question for many to answer so let's just put in the easy answers.

> A government is the man-made system that sets and administers "public policy," and then exercises executive, political and sovereign power through customs that mankind lived, as well as institutions mankind created, with the laws that the state wrote or follow orally. A government has many forms. Some of the most familiar to our current school of education are those governments we call democracy, republic, monarchy, aristocracy and dictatorships. And religion is a government too. Please know that truth.

What is the meaning of public written above? It means a community of people. A government in essence becomes the man-made vehicle that governs a community of people big or small.

Let's regress a bit and see how man made the world that we currently live in. What were the first innings of the game of life on planet earth, as we know the game?

Well, it started with one or two thoughts. The one energy divided into two equal halves. God has told me that our story, not man-made story, which we call history, began with a thought.

A first thought, by, as well as from God. Today, we call it the explosion that set off the Big Bang Theory. It was a fart, gas that came out and set in motion the explosion we call the creation of life. I see it began as a thought. So, we as a consciousness, keep dividing, as a run- away cell. We are now too many parts, each fighting the other to the point where we have lost our essence, not just our souls. It needs to stop.

Greatest example is the grandchildren of Queen Victoria. Three bad monsters. They believed they had God's permission to kill and maim. The three were the King of Britain, the Kaiser of Germany and the Czar of Russia. These three first cousins had a family feud that we call World War 1. This feud killed or caused the deaths of fifty million people in the first twenty years of the 20th century. Plus, all the nonsense going on today because of this WASP inbreeding.

The Story of Creation

As what I believe, the original myth of Satan illustrates; part of God, whom the various religions call Satan, the fallen angel, said to God: *"What if I created a way to have offspring and gave them a physical playground to live and experience physical life? Where creation can touch each other and feel each other, as well as see each other's physical costume of that dimension which I will create? The offspring, which I call children I will create, will need energy to move. This, I will call light. With light, they must have motor skills, so they can move around and make sure they get the light-energy to move and grow. So, what will I create?"*

God said, *"How about if I create a physical existence that can just sit and flow in the wind and the sun. But for creation to work, I must first create organic chemicals, or building blocks that with the light become alive."* Today we call this energy the Holy Ghost: The life force.

Satan said I want more. *"How about this? I will give these children a consciousness and let them co-create with me."* Creation will evolve God thoughts in a physical world that thought creates. And creations listen and became co-creators with God. As consciousness grew in this created physical space, some just stayed where they were as plants. Others need motion and so begin the life of first Pisces, the fish and sea creatures; then animals that could walk on land and breathe the air. Evolution of the unseen thoughts taught the animals to become mammals. Evolution taught creation how to reproduce, how to continue to grow, and finally, how to use the seven thoughts of our souls inside one body that I wrote about before.

The bible tells the story of creation in Genesis. But the current version says it occurred in seven days. But whose seven days? Not earth, as there was no earth. And what is a day? A day we define as how long it takes for this planet to circle around the sun- or energy force. Not every day is 24 earth hours.

How about we look at the Bible and see the book of Genesis as seven moments of creation? An opera of God's love. Creation is love. Life is creation and we shall not put a face on it. God is everything and everything is more than a mask we call a face.

Put a face on it, try to own it and then creation goes bye-bye, and you become a substance that wishes to live in only the past. You are then a memory of consciousness that runs backwards. By living, you create memories to treasure forever back in the non-physical world. The netherworld, which I refer to as the matrix, is where we all return to when our earth bodies physically die.

We do not die. We live our world here and return to figure out what's next. I explain this in detail in my book *"Sacred Knowledge: A Rock N Rollers Guide to Higher Consciousness."*

Remember before the world that exists now, everything was new and not tried. So, life on earth is one non-stop Jazz musical movement. Of sounds that become light and then take physical forms dictated by what our consciousness wants.

The human may be the current top consciousness on earth. Or maybe not. Dolphins are pretty spiritual too. The co-creator that keeps creating and letting other consciousness live in a much more predictable space. But know we are not God. We are from God, but we are not God, and God is our father, and it is to God whom we must live and respect. You cannot lie to God, for all you then become is a Pinocchio. God wants living children, not puppets on other living beast's strings. When we live in, and with truth, you will have God's love moving with you.

The seven days of our universe creation translated into seven separate moments in time.

> The overture: Day begins. Track one is the one when God creates light, which God created by thought from the emptiness that surrounds Gods Nirvana. Nirvana is existence at a zero state. Thought is where light begins. Explosions of second thoughts created players who create the matrix that gets translated into a blue print of physical reality.
>
> Truth! The Big Bang Theory of creation began. And this bang of creation still goes on today, creating new worlds and universes and life form on a truly endless space. Space thoughts created from the black holes of emptiness.
>
> Dawn: Track Two: God creates the universe we see. This is what the bible called the firmament. We call this heaven, but we are misled and think heaven is elsewhere, when the heaven of the bible refers to the creating the air that we breathe and giving it a gravitational force (GF). A GF

designed so the air stays below on earth and above earth creating the arc of earth, the land, the seas, as well as censors the strength of the sun light, so we can become life with the sun's energy force.

When I was a young man flying the Concord, I saw this design. It was so beautiful, and I used to hear this, is from all earth life. Man must protect this shield and the land and the seas below, or life, as you know it, will end. I did not understand then as I do now.

You see I am addicted to life and motion. I used music to be my magic carpet to get me around the world. Knowledge and living life as I did gave me the wisdom to try and open mankind's eyes. This book is being written because I love God, and I do love all of God's creations, and if we do not take a breath and teach eternal truths-God's law, we will all cease to exist in this dimension. And God will then have to create a new heaven for God's children to play in and learn love in all aspects of creation and perpetuation, as well as destruction.

All I want is to be able to learn to play the game of life with love, and share the love I have. I love life. No matter what the cards dealt me have been. I have learned to survive.

> The morning: Track Three: God creates here on earth the land and the sea. And God then creates the vegetation that breathes in the carbon chemicals now with life inside the neutron. After breathing in the carbon and changing the compound, the plant releases/exhales air to

continue the game of creation. Now there is an excess of oxygen, which becomes the building block for other forms of life.

God created every tree and plant and according to the consciousness that incarnate with the life force to be that plant. Then God created the ability to reproduce on their own, so they do not die when the life force leaves the body suit, the consciousness lives in physical form.

Mid day-high noon: Track Four. With the light overhead, this fourth movement is where God creates the physical forms that give us on earth the environment to become more then we currently are, living in the plant's Garden of Eden. Those substances, which also rotate around our sun, now with gravity that keeps them in their new-found shapes, are the names of the days of our week.

So, let me now share this knowledge with you. Why? Because these physical shapes were created in this movement. And in our past, schools were created to teach creation, and those schools taught why the seven objects were created by God to help us live and thrive in the physical, but not eternal matrix we call earth, our physical home.

Sunday is named after the light that gives us the energy force. That light is what we call the Sun. This star is the sun energy of God. People called this energy Zeus, Ra, or Jesus.

God created the moon that we call Monday. The moon is there to stop earth from getting too much sun that will blind life and burn us out. God created the planets and moons to rotate around each other so there would be light and dark during each rotation of the material around the sun. Our moon reflects the sun and teaches us to reflect and utilize the light we have properly. Not to kill each other, and be the biggest bully on our planet and Universe, but to share our knowledge and use our wisdom to keep creation alive for our father, God, and to honor our mother Earth is the matrix/womb of our lives in physical form.

Tuesday is named after Mars, that was created from the iron we need to make our blood work. Gives us the strength to move about and not fall into gravity's pull.

Wednesday is named after Mercury. The planet/runner who is closest to the sun (son), our energy. And Mercury in sacred knowledge will bring you the message.

Jupiter is Thursday. The sign of knowledge. The planet that creates a space for all the organic chemicals to sit and hide out in gas and liquid form, known as the moons of Jupiter.

Friday is what we call the morning or evening star, Venus. We on earth can see it at times in the morning sky, and other times in the evening sky. The star-planet that was created so we could see the beauty of the star in the morning of day. By looking at this star, we could understand the perils of desire when the star-planet appears in our view at different times at night.

The biggest gravitational mass in our universe is Saturn. The wisest planet: For here, all the seeds of chemical creation live. It has the greatest gravitational force on our universe. The moons of Saturn are rainbows of gases and liquids that really look like the seven colors of the rainbow. "A lot of sevens in creation," I hear you say. Yes, there is. Remember, we have seven wheels inside our physical body that make our body work. Those wheels are called chakras and when balanced, those chakras give off the colors of the rainbow, with red being one, and purple being seven. We call those vibrations lights aura.

Saturn, in sacred schools of training during what our current schools call "pre-history time," was changed to Satan. Satan became the dark force that kept consciousness imprisoned in deep density, so mankind forgets that man lives in both the physical and spiritual world. Satan is gravity. A gravity that locks you up in a physical space.

We then forget God, and make human gods to win and control our thoughts of life. So we can possess the physical.

The devil, as opposed to Satan in these sacred schools, was desire. If desire was not checked, you would do things that God did not want you to do. Venus, the evening star, became the planet of desire, represented by the devil. And Venus's name comes because during the day, she was love, sex and fertility. But too much love becomes desire, and the devil takes over. Get it?

Sacred schools in early earth times taught these truths. We call the world prehistoric, meaning before written history, because those in control want you to believe their way of owning our thoughts and minds is how God wanted it. Our ancestors worshiped nature. They worshiped different energies of God, knowing that they all add up to God. Today we are taught that this is paganism, and respecting earth is wrong. It is our mother. My friends, this is the age of information and that game will be over. I will now carry on.

> Evening is movement five. There is two parts to evening. First part is when the sun goes down. Earth changes. And with this darkness, part two begins. God created oceans that move to the motion of the moon. And God, during the sunset, filled the seven seas with animals and the air with birds.

> Then movement six, which is now the evening of the composition of the creation of earth. And in this universe, God created the land and the animals, and the bible now says God created man in God's own image. Not what the bible was supposed to say. It originally said; God created man by hand from the sand and gave man breath to live in this higher form here on earth. We are the only creation of God's hands and breath.

I told you before how and why man twisted the five-pointed star to being God, and us having five points being created to look like God. All lies.

And God only wishes for us to love God, not worship him. Be God's children and accept that fact. Not play

God and take control. Make rules that are not from heaven and create lies, saying God told you and your crew to take charge. Some of us speak with God, and those that really do know God, know that God tells you, in a small internal heart felt voice, to love and teach mankind, and to share and take responsibility for what you yourself do here on earth.

By the way, what I just said can be found in the Dead Sea Scrolls and was part of the bible before the book was rewritten. It appears in the Hebrew bible, which is not the Jewish bible. There is a big difference. A Hebrew chooses God; it is a present, active move. It does not end, it only grows. A Jew believes that God chose them. Big difference.

> The final movement is night. When creation is asked to rest, reflect and figure out what's next.
>
> Night, or sleep time, is when our consciousness does leave our bodies with a metaphysical hold, called a string attached, so we can return and live out the physical life. Remember, we are locked inside the body until released from that creation. Released, I must add, when the heart stops. The battery of physical life.
>
> When we sleep, it is our bodies that re-charge, and our consciousness dreams once again--like it will full time when we "die" here on earth. That is when we return to the matrix of creation.

This is what I believe. God, the whole, did not create us. God, the sun did. And we are all and we are all from the same team. The team of Hu-Man. Mankind here on earth.

Consciousness the son/sun of God.

I say this because now we must examine how Team Human, from consciousness, must live here on earth. How do we make the world a place for all to pursue happiness, as promised in the United British colonies' Declaration of Independence?

A thought reduced to writing by one of my now favorite spirits, Thomas Jefferson. Probably the greatest declaration written by mankind. In it is the message of communal and individual life.

We must build communities that teach and prepare all to have life, liberty, and to be able to pursue individual goals and create happiness. And Jefferson, like us all, was a man of contradiction, for he owned people's lives, as well as all their sperm and eggs. Jefferson knew this was wrong.

Where did we mankind go off course and become a rabid, angry dog? No longer one member of the pack. When did we become me, me, me? No longer we and me?

Our Constitution of 1788 twisted the message. The change was no longer God's government. The pursuit of happiness was changed to protect property first. Whose property? The peoples', or the individual's property. And who then and there could own the property?

What is property? This whole evolving concept; we need to redefine it for 2018. And I will, as we carry on.

I hear Jefferson in my heart tell me he wrote the Dream of Creation, but he and his co-conspirators to the British Empire, and to us, our founding fathers were not ready to live the dream. A society, not ready to live with true egalitarian beliefs, got in the way. The people were not ready. There was too much brainwashing thoughts of religions and governments. These, in essence, were the white European class, mixed with slaves and native Indians, and women with no rights. Question is what did these settlers learned about building a new land? The WASP's (white Anglo Saxon Protestant) called them savages. Creating a community of equals, with a world of absolute equal opportunity for all who wish to participate in their community was not for them. Not for them was equity for all.

So, what happens then? What did we do in 1787-88?

We begin the editing of our living consciousness. We created a constitution that allowed our nation to live and work with other nations, putting property and property owners in front of others. We built the same European order we said we wanted no part of. We had slave owners running a land to get their freedom from a King and Pope. Not to give freedom to all of mankind.

We chickened out of building a new world order.

I personally love baseball, and to understand the game, you must know what went on in the innings before you. That is why it is so important to follow me as I walk you down memory lane.

How did we get to where we are now as a nation? And what message do we give to the world? America is a game, and to understand who we are, we must know what we came from. So history, with judgment, but without conviction is needed. We must understand how the mantra of the Declaration got twisted in a war between the have-nots by statutes. Man-made rules, protecting the few, at the expense of everyone. We had a Bill of Rights guaranteeing political rights. But there was, and still is, no economic bill of rights guaranteeing health, welfare and safety to grow and prosper in a country living with God.

The promise that this nation would be a world of equality was put on hold, and we rejoined the world banking and religious order of material first, and God in the next life. We actually wrote slavery into our constitution, and took women out as equals.

Most did not care, as those living then had their farms to grow and lands to sow so they could feed their families. But things change, and we have gone through a few different lifestyles.

We went through the Industrial Revolution where we learned to play alchemy with living things and change gas to liquid or solids, and solids to gas or liquids, and liquids to gas or solids. We built a new world and people with this new order got new ministerial jobs and as things progressed and machines took over, lost those jobs and purpose.

Our nation then was based on the WASP version of Christianity. So, let's go back to the mindset of those living in 1788 and how they worshipped the man-made god of those times.

Remember, you can take religion out of government, for religion is man-made order. You cannot remove God, as we are all part of the one God. We are God's thoughts in living, physical independent form.

So, if we believe we are doing what God wants us to do, then let's review the Bible and its Rules;

The Ten Commandments:

Our first government of equals?

These commandments were given to build a community of equals living then in what was called the Levant. In the bible, we are told how to create a living community world that honors God. We are told to live by these commandments, which were applicable to the Hebrews. Hebrews being those who chose God.

But now I must share what a Hebrew was then. Hebrew was their word for people then living in Egypt. These people thought they were the only people. They did not know the world that existed. They knew their living world.

There were no Egyptian people, as they called themselves Hebrews. The Hebrews had a class-caste system. Moses, the living character, fled with the Hebrews, stealing gold from the slave owners, as the slaves fled to create a new world based on one God. The God of all. In Egypt, everyone worked for the

Priests who controlled life, and had their puppet Pharaoh, as the ruler of their house.

The people of Abraham's tribe also choose God, they said. They did not wish to live and be bossed around by all the lesser gods of the then ruling "Egyptians", as well as other Near Eastern powers. They wished to build a land based on equality. Whose equality?

Remember there were people already living on the land today we call Israel. So, Moses and his people invaded and took the land from those who did not choose their God, the Hebrew God.

This is important. The Promised Land, I believe was one where all mankind, then called Hebrews by the Hebrews, would live in peace and harmony with the one God as their moral compass. The Ten Commandments were the guiding light.

No one was excluded in promised land space. All land is God's space. All humans must learn to live together and in agreed harmony.

I now hear as I am writing,

"All the space was promised to mankind whom I created with my hands and my breath to live as my children and build a living physical heaven. I did not authorize anyone to take and possess for themselves anything. I authorized mankind to share, and build, not to me, but for me. Be happy sharing, my children, and I will be so happy you figured it all out."

I just channeled that.

If I may, let's look at these ten building blocks to create society so we can all have the promises of community. A community of mankind's team that creates their government to be:

1. For the People
2. Of the People
3. By the People

A community where we all can live life with equality that allows each the opportunity to pursue their happiness based on real living justice for all.

Remember, God is all the colors of our rainbow, and we must protect and allow each color of mankind, and all life to live, with equal opportunity, their individual dream. That is, and this is most important, as long as they take part in sharing earth.

The first commandment we are told was the following: You shall have no other gods before me. This I feel, was a response to what we humans were doing, making man-made gods, living the mammon life. Really giving away our living energy to those illusions of gods instead of sharing our energy with life here on earth.

Please remember the following:

- We, the Hebrews, chose God
- God did not choose us over anyone else, and
- God did create all of us, so we are ALL God's children.

The Second Commandment: You shall make no idols. Means no one is better than you. Do not give away your power to anyone. Live your life and share it. Once, my life was made making false gods. I knew what I was doing, but I was raised believing it's a living thing. I was wrong.

Those life experiences shaped me. Let me be who I am. Without these experiences I would not have the wisdom to seek the truth and share it with you. I hate no one that I have come into contact with. Even the person called "Lean," that created the storm that took my son's life. I, once again, was encouraging creating an image of a human being better than others. I paid for my games. I so miss my son, but God says to me, *"You will see Barron soon enough, and for eternity. Live and do what you're doing. It is your path. You survived. Please help others thrive by sharing the life you lived and the lessons you learned."*

The Third Commandment: You shall not take the name of the LORD, your God, in vain. What does vain mean in this sentence? Lord is the boss, so what is vain? Well, vain means you take the object, which could be you or something else, and have an excessively high appearance of that object.

Here on earth, we are not nouns, as we are taught, we are verbs. We are alive, and as living beings, we are action and moving. So is God. God is not dead and when we grow, so does God. Because we have free will to live life, and that is what our LORD gave us all. We must not make our God the God who instructs us, as individuals, on what to tell and make others do on their individual path to happiness. On the collective path, we must remember we are just one raindrop in the sea of consciousness and we must honor all god's creation, not just ourselves.

The Fourth Commandment: Remember the Sabbath day, to keep it holy. Here, this made sense back then. It was a means to get the community of "farmers" to get together in a "church" so the community of all can share the information they learned from the West and the North and the East and the South. The true spiritual cross of mankind with the church was really a community center, in the center of the community, as a positive, not a cross to kill others on.

The Hebrew word for holy is *qodesh*. This word means apartness, sacredness. So, what we are told to do is set apart time in what they then called the Sabbath to be with God. God is in all our hearts. Listen to your heart and you will hear the beat of God's drums. Let your antenna in your brain bring the vibrations of higher spirit into you. But to hear God, listen to the beat of your heart, and beyond those drums is the voice. Listen for it, and then for the voice, and you will hear God talk to you.

I learned this the hard way. Fighting this truth. Living life and misleading people into believing the artists I worked with, or the movie I was working on, held the answers for your future life. The truth is, YOU hold the answers. No one else has the exclusive ownership. I read Yoginama's autobiography and reread the portion endless times of how he meets God as the Yogi's spirit instructed me to do. Why? So I could finally meet God and get to know God. It worked and now I share this truth with all of you.

The Fifth Commandment: Honor your mother and father. Notice how mother is written first. But we have two mothers. The first is our individual mother. For it is these humans, men with wombs, that bring us into physical life here on earth. Even for themselves. We must protect them so they can bear children, as children are really the only assets that belong to man. The rest of earth's assets we must share. And we must honor our co-creators, as we do God, our creator. But saying that, we must remember that our physical mother and father must respect us. But the truth is this clause means so much more and I will get to it real soon.

The Sixth Commandment: You shall not murder. And murder is what we do. We create man-made Gods, give those man-made Gods' a religion, their own sport of sorts, a breach of the first and second commandment, and say that our new God wants us to kill. We create countries that say we live under God and God says it's ok to kill. God never, ever, said that, or used those thoughts. Those thoughts are dark energy that light must remove from your heads. We even get others to believe it and live it. This must stop. And why do we kill? To steal material. So we create a world separate from God, and say our man-made God, made in our image, says war for personal profit is justified. This is the worship of mammon.

The Seventh Commandment: You shall not commit adultery. True. Why would anyone? Please note, one who cheats on others will cheat on you too. I learned this truth the hard way. Someone who I came to be close with was the mistress of someone who was very married, and lied. I came on as a hero and did not understand the lyrics to one of my favorite Beach Boys songs, *"Here Today."*

> *"Be no one's mistress, if that party cannot live in truth then why live with them."*

This is what I believe the commandment means. We can get divorced and move on, but living a lie to get more, and cheating, and not living in truth on others whom we swore allegiance to, and owe transparency too, is wrong behavior.

The Eighth Commandment: You shall not steal. God is watching you. And all your man-made laws notwithstanding, taking what is not yours is wrong. Stealing is when you take something that you know is not yours. It is not taking what you believe is yours. Big difference. This is where man-made laws must apply to decide who has a larger living claim to possess. But just taking because you want is wrong, and society must stop this errant thought. There is plenty for everyone. Everyone can be their own king here in heaven, as long as they learn to share with others.

Today the American Foreign policy is dictated by third party private bankers, and what they can take using the military of America as its force. Sort of similar to what the Vatican did with their Spanish conquistadors. Those holy warriors came to steal and destroy the knowledge and cultures of those living then and there in the Western Hemisphere. Really rewriting man's life experience and making it their history. Not the full story of mankind. Get it?

The Ninth Commandment: You shall not bear false witness against your neighbor. In essence you shall not lie. We are God's children not Pinocchio's. In today's world, we have a system in place that is all lies. Just look at your contracts with banks. Look at your deals with your appliance companies. Your insurance. Your politicians who promise one thing and lie for your vote. Why have we the electorate never sued a politician for breach of contract? Why do we not hold anyone accountable? We are raised to lie and it must stop, or we will be stopped. We will kill each other off.

The Tenth Commandment: You shall not covet. This one is so important and allows for entrepreneurship to create but makes you question where people who say they are Christians ever came up with the game called Banker's capitalism.

What is covet? My understanding is the following: "to desire wrongfully, inordinately, or without due regard for the rights of others." The best example is, in essence, the entire underlying philosophy of the British-American Imperial foreign policy today.

We steal and we desire the materials that other nations have under their land. Our system is really based on accumulating resources for private profit by dispossessing others who live on the land, of those resources.

These physical and material resources that nature buried for a reason are what the controllers of our society now wish to bring to the surface and release into the air. That release in the air will continue to change the entire composition of the balance on earth that lets today's species, not just man, to live and survive as well as prosper on our path to happiness

Happiness, as an individual and as a member of a family, a community, a town, a city, a county, a state, a nation, a continent, a world of life that must share the globe. We must teach and make these few understand, with consequences attached, that no real living God says take from this area, as they are savages and do not need, and you can have more. This is wrong, and we need to listen to God's rules.

In the Ten Commandments that were given by God, the one God of the Hebrews, gave us eight rules of what not to do building communities out of sand. God also gave us two commandments as to what we should do.

And please note that all three-Middle East religions, Judaism, Christianity and Islam, begin as Hebrews, with Abraham. But like the Queen Victoria in the UK, whose grandsons as rulers in three lands started World War I, the grandchildren of Abraham wanted ownership and control, so the grandchildren all created new versions of the one God.

Again, I repeat, the grandchildren, and further generations of Abrahams came and wanted their own God, so the original bible became three bibles, teaching our God is better than yours. Really sick and distorted behavior. God gave us free will. There is no destiny. God created us to see what God's children will do.

So, to recap, these are God's fouls. When we commit one of these aggressions, a foul, we have a score against our souls as well as the essence of mankind.

One, we all must learn the reasons why we did it, so when circumstances happen again. Part two, we do not commit the same foul.

Recapping the above. The eight No's:

1. You shall have no other gods before me.
2. You shall make no idols.
3. You shall not take the name of the Lord, your God, in vain.
4. You shall not murder.
5. You shall not commit adultery.
6. You shall not steal.
7. You shall not bear false witness against your neighbor.
8. You shall not covet.

Imagine if we honored those ground rules of the sport of life as God wishes. What a wonderful world this will be.

Listen to two songs if you can. The first one is *"I believe"* and the second is *"What a Wonderful World"*. Inspiration and timeless. Art is the key to keep building and us moving. But when we change nature with our art we must constantly review and see what the changes have done to our playing field. Our playing field is three levels; our basement, which is underground, our ground level, and our penthouse, the sky. It needs to stay balanced.

To do this there are two commandments that require you to do something. Those two are:

1. Honor your mother and father.
2. Remember the Sabbath day to keep it holy.

I reverse the order because in this 21st century, what I feel it really means, is that we must respect those who made our living world. Our parents and their generation did this. But respect is not obedience. Respect is sharing what you see and what you feel, and your elders must respect you too. We do not know everything, life is a team sport, and we must share it. The most important thing to remember is the Sabbath, your communion with God.

> God lives in your heart. You do not need an organization to reach and speak with God. Nor a set day of the week.

Any day, any hour you feel the need to reach out and speak to your maker, God is always there for you. Keep your time of the day or days of communion with God pure and straight up. Do not lie to God. Tell God what's up and ask for God's advice.

This is a never-ending learning process. It is the goal of mankind to live not just learn.

And as I wrote everything you just read, I heard that honor your mother and father is about living with God and protecting mother earth. Everyone's mother and father. This is the real meaning of those two commandments.

> The sacred meaning of honor your mother and father is one which becomes our role as the elders, to insure and make our communities understand. It is about we, it is not just about me.

Now let me take you on a journey to live in the 21st century.

> The government we must create, so we can all not just survive, but also have the opportunity to thrive and live the dream that we incarnated to have in physical reality here on earth, is dictated by our past.

If we learn not just what happened, but also why moves were made in the chess game of life, it can show us how we can win and create a better world for our heirs.

Remember, to play this game of life, we need a board, and if we screw up the board that we live in, and on called earth, which is all three levels of earth, we will only have our matrix creations in new non-earth physical form. These forms, incarnating on their new planet product, called bodies. Bodies suited to survive this new dimension's physical universe.

Community

1. What is a community?
2. Who does the community serve?
3. What does serve mean?
4. Is the community built to serve an individual or group(s)?
5. What constitutes a group, and when does that group become a community?
6. What are the reasons that people become a group?
7. What does a group do?
8. How does a group work?
9. What holds a group together?
10. What happens when the currency that put a group together ends?
11. What happens when the group grows and outgrows its boundaries that created the group?
12. How does one make the rules that run the group? Who runs the group?
13. What is currency? Is it only material, or can it also be knowledge and tradition?
14. What gives the currency value?
15. Who owns knowledge?
16. Knowledge for who and what?
17. Is there a difference between knowledge for individual enjoyment and knowledge to build and keep a community alive as well as growing?
18. When does a government of equal networks become a government of hierarchy and control?
19. What is the difference in those two types of governments?

20. Does the one God play a role in man-made communities and man-made religions?
21. What is the role that God wants us to be governing by?
22. Does the past rule us or guide us?
23. Is life about growing and becoming more? Or staying and living by the rules of our ancestors not just the guidelines God gave us in the Ten Commandments we say we believe in?
24. How do we build a 21st century government that works for all the people, not just the few?
25. Must government change to reflect the new earth times?
26. What are the real goals of humans and how do we get there to this higher ground of living in and on this planet.

I have had trouble sitting and writing this section. I have done my reading and my living. I was ready to download and go. However, I was stopped.

Stopped by whom? Stopped by God and higher consciousness, as well as my ancestors, our ancestors. How was I stopped? Communications in my head and visions at night in my sleep. This is my spiritual insomnia.

The insomnia was not to go to sleep. It was not tossing and turning at night. No, no, no. I went into a void and came out and saw moves to make to change the game of life the way we are played, to let others own our living energy.

I love people. I love a smile. I love people trying and winning their personal battle. I love teams. I love dreams. I love art. Art, in all of the physical and spiritual arts forms that we here on earth can share.

Life is Art. It must come from the heart and must be sustainable here on earth as earth is our playground.

We must understand that this game is like baseball except for one big difference. Like baseball, we humans start the game by pitching our wants and needs to earth. We run the field and hope earth allows us to stay on the field. A playing field really of our consciousness dreams. A field that for some may become nightmares, when a community does not stop the harm done by the few on the whole.

> "If we push earth too far, give earth a pitch it chooses to hit, earth may choose to not hit the pitch alone. Earth may choose to remove us from earth's field. We need to realize this truth"

We need to have governments that protect the health and welfare of we the people, and earth too. As earth is the maternal parent we must respect. We need to make sure that our moves are safe while we start the moves, and analyze the moves as they continue, to see what we are doing to each other as well as earth itself as the moves continue.

Earth first, my friends. And the burden of proof to continue our actions of change must be on us when we change the playing field God and Mother earth gave us to live in this earth-oxygen body. We can not just go on believing earth is for mankind, and that all living things create the balance for mankind and mankind alone that allows us to exist here on earth.

Thomas Jefferson himself said rules must be reviewed every twenty years to see how the rules fit in the ever-changing world of life. Jefferson was not a fan of our Constitution, but understood.

The US Constitution of 1788/89 changed the Articles of Confederation. The Article's rules and regulations ran our nation for our first eight years. We were a network of equals. No central controlling force making our orbit go this way or that way.

The constitution is our sun and it controls the spirit of our orbit as a nation. And those who control the ship control our nation? Those that control our nation are those who control our currency that we take in exchange for our time, energy and possessions to sell, as well as buy.

The US Constitution is 229 years plus old. It is long overdue for a reboot. Those rules were for a land-based society of 2,500,00 people. Not the 360,000,000+ people we have today living in, what we call, the age of information. What our prophets called the age of Aquarius.

Thomas Jefferson who was not a fan of this new game, but understood the need then and there for this type of government amongst a fraternity of Kingdoms, and the Pope said we must change our rules every twenty years, so our rules fit the living in essence, not the dearly departed. The game is to keep alive the eternal optimism that we are a land for everyone, not just the few.

To do this, everyone must control the currency. To make change, my friends, we must nationalize the Fed and give the power back to those we elect. Not let others consult us, and make believe for public appearances that they listen to our needs, while they act for their needs to own and control our living souls.

This is my Columba since my awakening as a worldly renaissance man.

September 9th 2017, and the Hurricane Irma is coming to Florida. I choose to come back to Miami from NY because I really wanted to be alone with God. I wanted to continue writing my thoughts now contained in this book. I wanted to commune with God and learn about the anger earth was unleashing on us. And why we make it worse. Why we cannot get our collective, let alone our individual act together. I meditated, and this is what I heard to share with all.

I heard a message to go back and review in your awareness, to Egypt, and discuss how government for the people themselves began. Go to the man you people call Moses. See what he did, and that what he did was not what I asked him to do.

> *"Moses broke the entire do-not commandments. In fact, did you ever ask yourself if it was I who give it to him? Or some lesser energy that created these no's."*

As you read the past as mankind has written in his-story, the story unfolds into the following that I heard:

"The Hebrews were the names that Egyptians called themselves back in those days. So, the Egyptians were running away from Africa---Egypt, and crossed the Red Sea that no God needs to open. You know that, as you have been to the Red Sea with your son Barron."

"You saw truth then. You investigated and learned a lot. I never chose just the Hebrews of Egypt. I created everything and more. I am. And you say you are ready to speak truth to power and fight the power to help people become aware of the truths. Well, continue writing."

I did say choose me and I will be there for you. Words of that era for those then living, whom you follow their thoughts today. That meant be a Hebrew. Choose me.

"Tell people the truth. Abraham and his early flock from a location they called Urn, chose me. They remembered me. And when you allow me to be present in your heart as a guiding force, I will guide you. But when you use my name in vain and claim that I promise to be your God, and deliver your land from others living there, no, it's on you. When you then attack and kill using my name, this is wrong, and again it's on you. Mankind of all ages has used my name in vain and peace will never occur until everyone stops his or her madness."

"Moses broke all the commandments of what he was not to do. He was a leader living in darkness. Peace is the answer. You are all my children. All."

"Tell people a government must work to build community. It must support all the community, and everyone must have access to live their dream. The dream must be where they are prepared to work towards getting it without murder, theft, adultery, coveting, and no idolatry. People need to stop being dishonest. Work for the common good. Save the land and honor your mother earth by preserving and conserving. Do not waste for your generation earth. Remember you are custodians for the future you's."

"You see, son, inducing fear allows those who make the fear to create their control by removing the fear they created." Simple game: Fear of things that others control and make you worried bad things will happen to you. The dark energy then offers you a solution. That solution gives us power and we will stop the fear!!

"You have two bodies. One is physical and was given to you by Mother earth and me. The other body is astral, the matrix, and it does not come from me. It is I. It is me being you. Running away from me. Trying to be your own God."

*You, as an existence, too, can get a cancer. The bacteria that causes spiritual cancer is fear. And when it engulfs your entire individual essence, it is called hate. Hate, like a cancer grows, and must be **extinguished**. I gave you all free will and I watch and wait for you all to figure it out.*

"Get rid of fear by teaching--not dictating--the truth to people. Tell them who you are. Finish

> *this book and give them the outlines for the 21st Century Government as you call it, based on the sacred truths you hold so dear to your heart and soul. Undo the hate by walking with the light, Steven. Be my son. You are not Pinocchio. The ultimate power is to be love, not to be able to control. Help my children, the people grow again and prosper. State your views."*

I now hear or feel different energies that say we will take it from here. It starts with the first constitution in Athens, which was written as rap song. The man's name was Solon. He was an Athenian statesman of 600 B.C. Solon was a lawmaker and poet. He is remembered for those who research his past as a man who legislated against the moral decline of the few property owners trying to control everyone, rich or slave.

> *"Steven, you are the man of music. You hear the vibrations of love and have learned the lower energy of fear and then hate. Sing your truth and just be you. You are ready my son, and I will be watching and supporting you."*

I awoke. And fell out of bed. Sweating, and determined to carry on and finish this tome.

Building community for everyone to pursue happiness. How do people live together?

Simple, we do what other animals do, we create a ruling order.

Ever really watch the birds? They move as a flock. When they land, it is each for their own. They get food and feed their families when they sit still.

Fish move in groups. Bees move in groups. Plants share soil. They work together and the wisest survives. Not the biggest or strongest. Those that grow too much and disrespect the balance end up dead and gone.

Nature

Universal truths. We are nature in this body form. Our consciousness may come from beyond but in this life, we must defend nature, not try to change it for our own purpose and desire. Nature will fight back.

I Promise.

I went through the Hurricane called Irma. Learned many things. We are told it was bigger and badder than any recorded hurricane before. Badder because it lingers and causes more damage to this pest that destroys earth. The pest is man.

Many years ago, while I was growing up, there was a song sung by a band called Quicksilver Messenger Service.

Their song is called *"What About Me."*

The song begins with the following lyrics:

> *"You poisoned my sweetwater*
> *You cut down my green trees*
> *The food you feed my children*
> *Was the cause of their disease*
>
> *My world is slowly falling' down*

*And the airs' not good to breathe
And those of us who care enough
We have to do something."*

This was the late sixties. The *we* generation of my youth, became the *me* generation, and only worried about their *me*.

We fell asleep at the wheel. And look what we have done to earth. A few may have wealth in paper profits, but there is no health. And therefore, there is no wealth. Real wealth.

How do we protect us from each other's greed and fears?

- We create an order that polices as well as administers the necessities of our living life.
- This order becomes the system that ensures everyone has a function.
- That everyone has a proper living standard that participates in the community.
- And we encourage people to create the impossible dream to build a better world for all, not just them and maybe their personal family.

How do we do this?

We create a government for the people, by the people, and of the people of the community, so to be governed by this form of law and order.

Questions we now need to review.

Government

1. What is a Government?

- A government is a system that becomes the ruling order of whoever agrees to live under that system.

- A government has many subjects who in reality become the object of the government It can be your family. It can be your schools. It can be your sports teams and the leagues that set the rules and order for your team to play the sport.

- A government is a business. A religion is a government.

- I will now walk us through the types of governments that are so duly created.

There are three types of Governments. In fact, these governments existed at the time Jesus the man was born.

Same mental concepts just different times.

Let's review:

- One, Rulers and their so chosen order rule one. Requires a god to confirm. Man-made god, I must add.

- Two. By rules and regulations. Again, requires a man-made god that somehow says to the educated few, that these are the rules and regulations I insist you follow. Lies. If this was true, that means God has left our building.

- o Three. The people who choose their living leader. The elder. The elder is the coach of our living society. The coach oversees our game for all, not just for him, family and co-conspirators of society control. A dictator like Castro.

- Governments of the current world order mix these three concepts.

- But all people care about is how they survive in this world they fell into.

- We left God. And now what. Well, we learn to live our physical existence without God.

- The game of physical life.

- Government is created to maintain order. But whose order?

- Life is a play to see how we act when one of the three gains control of the community.

- Spirits create the play. We are the pawns. The Actors playing out the unscripted game.

Once a government is chosen, the game begins of who controls what. Then, once that is answered, stories are written to tell you why.

So, our current living game begins in the Euro-labeled 15th century.

And before I move on, we must understand the name Europe comes from. According the poet, Homer, the name comes from a mythological queen of Crete, the land of the Minoans. The Queens' name was Europa.

Man Made Governments

I must state that our current knowledge of government begins with the logic pounded out in the 17th and 18th century, so-called the Age of Enlightenment, or even its sister, called the Age of Reason. But it is in the fifteenth century that these seeds of current life were planted.

These intellectual few men who studied the past of their worlds, created a world based on dualism. A world of separation. The separation of Church and State. A world that is a lie, because we are all part of the energy of God, and you cannot separate God from your lives. You can remove religion as man-made religions, not God.

The game is to believe we can only create certainty through separating the parts. Being a team sports fan, I know that logic is wrong.

To win, and life is a sport where survival with growth is the win, one must get the team of life to move together. Not to believe that one is more important than the other. And if you like, see how many times teams with a home run champ win the World

Series. The answer is simple, it happens only when there is a team.

What the enlightened few did is, separate us in our language by backing the power of the subject over the aura of the object. Subject from object. Example being:

1. Males from females
2. Body from Spirit, and the big one,
3. Humans from nature.

Today separating us from the rest of nature has given us the physical but not spiritual ok to kill off other species and plants in record numbers, as we change the chemical and biological composition of earth for only our short-term gain.

Before I leave this thought control section, we must understand how the few WASP's in control of the Euro lands and the U.S. took the theory of evolution, which Darwin lifted from others and made it justify their so-called white man's burden to civilize the whole world into their new world order. This is a crime, and we must reign in the out-of-control tribes of Northern Europe who believe they are better than anyone else. White supremacy is total bunk.

The Vatican is not the only one who used their lies to take over our thoughts of creation, and who was chosen to rule those so created. We are all equally capable, at the beginning, to help build a better and more just world. For the living, and our heirs, as well as honor our ancestors who got us here.

That is the current war of our land. Are we kingdom, or pope, or equals? And, my friends, superman is the essence of our souls that will have a clean-up hitter to save our future days. Yes, I believe in fairy tales, for they do come true. The word fairy tales. used to be written faire. Fiare is a French word, and it means enchanted, not make believe, and can never come true.

We set the scene. We water our garden. Let's continue:

Again, government is a social contract. A social contract that exists by behavior. It is an agreement between the governed and those who serve the people in the peoples' government. We do not serve those who we elect. They must serve us.

Basic question. Who is the subject? Who is the object? The governed or those who govern?

Why do I ask?

Because the subject controls the object. And with the best of initial intentions our country is no longer the nation our founding fathers created. We were created to live the sacred knowledge. The sacred knowledge is earth, is a paradise when the people govern themselves, and do so honoring their mom, called earth, and their father, the creator

Our founding fathers knew this and said so in the Declaration of Independence, in 1776. The mantra is Life, Liberty and the Pursuit of Happiness. The mantra by man to God. Let us build a nation for all and God, we will honor you and Mother Earth. We will let people live and create in freedom, where everyone understands they can pursue their dreams and live life in happiness.

As John Lennon sang *"The world can live as one."* In peace and harmony, I must add.

But how?

- Give the people health, welfare and safety.
- Let those who need work, work for the community of mankind.
- Let the others----called "Type A" personalities, go out and create their own world order. But when that order gets too big, be prepared to bring it back to earth.

How are governments created? By people, or by force. And when people create governments, they do it for their living needs. And living on this globe is not the same everywhere. So, we create rules and procedures to help us survive our geographical locations.

Geographic cultures and their governments:

The 1400's Chinese had their encyclopedia. This series of books showed how to make many of their inventions, which ran their Chinese society. Examples being, gunpowder, a toy for them, and the printing press, as well as maps in detail of the whole world the Chinese explored and recorded. Again, these books were shared, so everyone could become aware of the Empire.

The Chinese gave euro man the books. Why? The living knowledge would make the Western world wish to join the east under Chinese supervision. The goal was to awe the west with knowledge, not physical force.

Their inventions did change our world, but not the way the Chinese wished. China, who in 1434, after a trip to Italy, had the biggest navy in the world, went back to China and closed down the navy. The Chinese realized that Europe was a lost cause, and their civilization needed to be saved from us Euro fools.

The Vatican tried to control the ownership of this knowledge but failed. The knowledge was a pandora's book to end the domination of the Vatican's dark ages.

The biggest invention we in the western world got and learned to use? The printing press. That first printing press changed their world, and we are still living that change.

The Europeans were able to read the bible in their own language. Not just hear others read them in Latin, the secret knowledge. This changed our world. Religious wars in Euro lands ensued, but first came the second major event.

That event was the Ottoman Turks taking over Constantinople. The Eastern Orthodox Church fled to a peninsula off Thessaloniki, Greece. This is where the sacred knowledge of the Orthodox Church is still hidden to this day.

If you are male, and wish a great trip of education, go to the Peninsula that is home to the Eastern Orthodox Church. Only men can go? Why? Because all religions derived from Abraham of the Middle East in their doctrines, remove women from active participation. We need to revisit this nonsense.

The Vatican got scared with the Islamic takeover of Eastern Europe waterways to the control of Asia Minor, and decided they would go takeover the territory that everyone in the know, knew about, called today the Western Hemisphere. The Vatican had the maps of the lands and they knew where the gold and silver was located in our Western hemisphere. Why?

Because the Incas were Chinese. The Chinese colonized this alleged new world. The name Peru is Chinese. Means mist. And the West coast of Peru has a misty rain. Get it?

The Vatican wanted in. The Vatican deputized the conquistadors of the land the Romans called Hispania, which we call today the Iberian Peninsula. The land of Portugal and Spain.

These soldiers, whom we call conquistadors, were told the Virgin Mary would calm the seas. They needed to spread the word to these uncivilized heathens and take the riches and fame for the Vatican and King, in the name of Vatican Christ.

These myths were created so that the Gladiators, the deputized Vatican soldiers, would help kill those living in this western world. Then the Vatican could create the new world for the Vatican. Get it?

The story of an individual named Christopher Columbus discovering a new world is a lie. This world existed and the name Christopher Columbus, put into Latin, and then translated back to English, is a pigeon carrying a message of the Vatican's version of Christ.

The Vatican set out to conquer the new world, and did so with their warriors in metal, the Spanish conquistadors. All one big game.

Yes, there was a captain of the ships. But a central figure named Christopher Columbus? Who had two names then and there? Those two names are a secret message when translated from Latin. The messenger bearing Christ.

The North Eastern part of the new world the Vatican wanted was the metals, including gold, and to find the fountain of youth. Look where they went. Not by accident, I must add. This search for the fountain of youth was really the attempt to find Atlantis, which the maps hidden in the Vatican's vaults were shown to be in the lands that came out of the Caribbean, the Florida Keys and today's Florida. Hence, the Spanish obsession with Florida.

The new world was to be just like the European World the Vatican created. The sacred knowledge was hidden. It became secret. Only the Vatican and those they choose would know the Columba of their true reason of their creation in the new world that the Vatican was going to make.

This New Vatican World was created to enforce the belief that "God has appointed the Vatican to rule the earth". Of course, they would enforce that the Vatican is the only direct line to communicate with God.

The Vatican tried to become the seven seas messenger of the rules and regulations of their manmade image of God. Their God, the one they called Christ, (Cristo in Latin, which, my friends, means the anointed one in Hebrew). Someone or thing anointed Jesus the man and a son of God to God.

The message was, behave and your next life will not be here on earth, you will be sitting with God in heaven. Those who do not respect our ruling order will forever languish in hell beneath your feet, and the earthman walks on you.

I was in Portobelo, Panama. A big slave point of the Vatican days of taking over the lands of Northern South America. The slaves would get off the ship and then go to Church and meet the statue of Jesus Christ. This statue of Jesus was black. Dressed in Purple robes, with gold attached as trinkets on the robe. The message is simple; these Africans were sold that the next life will be with you and the black Jesus. Shut up and serve, so you will get to meet Jesus Christ, our savoir. Yep, the one we now use to enslave you into our way of life. Sick.

Before I continue I feel I must share what sacred really means.

Sacred is a term of art that describes something that gives you the listener or the viewer. awareness and connection to your existence, be it here and now, or with the eternal. Your connection to creation. Your connection to God. The problem becomes what is God?

The sacred knowledge of why we are here is to build a world where we can share life as one God-created community. Where we each create our own worlds, called happiness, while allowing everyone the

opportunity to do so and the liberty to breathe. The government must provide for the health and wealth of the people, and secure their safety to make the sacred message work.

Thomas Jefferson, and his team, who helped him write and review and then publish the Declaration of Independence, knew this message. The Declaration was their Columba. Not the Vatican version. Which is why the Declaration says without kingdom or pope. The message is, we the people are the government. Words that the people were not ready to live. The coming mantra for all mankind.

We were to become a network of equal states that shared geography, to build a community of equality for all. We just needed to learn what all really meant. Knowledge and awareness are a moving of goal posts. It never ends.

The mascot of our young nation then was a woman, representing mother earth. Then, when we became a European imperialist, and war was our goal, around the time we entered World War 1, and sold war-bonds to finance a war, we became Uncle Sam. Mother Earth no longer mattered.

New game. Game of capitalism. Here it is in a nut shell. If our land did not have it, we would just steal it from elsewhere. Possession of property took control. With no God saying this theft is OK, let alone the right to kill and maim.

Back to the Vatican's conquest of their New World. Also note that two years after the fall of Constantinople in 1453, the Vatican issued an edict, a Papal Bull, authorizing the people of Hispania to buy African blacks and own them as slaves for their lives, as well as the lives they produce for all time. The reason? They needed a slave force to create the Agriculture empire for the Vatican's legions to live in luxury and slaves to mine the silver and gold.

The three commodities that the fall of Constantinople caused the Vatican to lose, were their Myrrh, Frankincense and Gold. This was their black gold and drugs, as well as the healing power of their day. In fact, it is what you will read the three kings of the Middle East brought to Jesus. With the Turks in Control of the Middle East, the Vatican, lost their source.

The true story, not his-tory of the Catholic Church will appear and be taught soon. It is not pretty, and it is not in line with Jesus and his preaching. In fact, the anti-Vatican Christ is Jesus.

Concerning the governments of Jerusalem in the Christian years, now known as BC1/AD1, there were three styles of governments:

Government Class 1 is called the Sadducees.

This was a government run by royalty-priests and passed down to their families. You had to be born into this crew or marry into it to be part of this crew.

Today this theory could be carried onto the Independent third-party Bankers who rule our world with the illusion that they own our currency. These Bankers come before the people.

Obama himself proved it when he gave them the money to distribute to the people to get out of the crash of 2008 they themselves created. Selling scams. But they were too big to fail, so we the people failed.

Obama was not a man of change. A man afraid to be the difference. In fact, it looks like he was owned and controlled by Wall Street. Truth., He was financed by Wall Street, and they paid for his schooling, too. If he was the man of the people, not just a great speaker, he would have had the balls to give the people the money direct from our treasury, and shut down once and for all the Federal Reserve Cartel that runs our nation.

Obama blinked and gave into the banks. The two presidents who tried to stop this independent scam in their time, Kennedy and Lincoln, both were shot dead. In full public execution style. Conspiracy theory my ass. Truth that simple.

The Priestly order of Bankers then did what Bankers today still do; they kept the money and lent it out with interest, as opposed to investing it for growth. Sad.

Government Class 11 is the Pharisees.

This group is educated into a system of rules that they enforce on all. It is an elite class which is self-appointed and self-perpetuating, too, I must add. This becomes the law system we have today. The system then was created because they said God told them of this order. Interesting. God gives you free will. Not rules and regulations. Recommendations, as in the Ten Commandments, but not demands which are commands, or else. We are here to figure it out.

It is here, at times, where the first-class merges into the second class. What they do is to split the spiritual side for the priest and the earth side for the lawyers of the lands in our world today. But straight up, you cannot take God out of the earth equation. When you do, you get the disorder we have today.

But you can remove religion, as God did not create religion. Man did. Our founders knew this truth.

The Truth is - who made up all these rules, and why do we believe them to be true? And, by believing them to be true, we make them true.

Government Class 111 was the Essenes.

The group was made of people running their own society by merit, and based on equality. Jesus became one of the spiritual leaders. This is how life should be. A government that runs itself by the people, for the people and by the people.

The new world of 1492, really the Western Hemisphere, copied these three ruling orders of societies before the arrival of the Vatican and the other sea-faring Euro Men.

In the South, you had empires of rulers. A priestly hierarchy order.

In the North you had federations, networks of essences, who shared the land and the government responsibilities between the people and themselves.

The European world was about to change, and so would their version of government. New combinations of class one and two would appear, until the US tried to do two and three. Here is our story. No longer his/ story.

This is what happened to our nation with the invention and then implementation of our US Constitution back in 1789. This constitution hid the sacred knowledge as the world was not yet ready to live in a world based on equality. No, we were to live in a world based on property ownership. A world that our declaration said was wrong. A world without separate kingdom or pope.

Remember, as I repeat, man-made religion, and God made man. In Church they say Amen, which, my friends, means men again.

We need to live with God, and honor Mother Earth. That is why our nation's capital is called the District of Columbia. Our Columba is *we the people living here, and honoring Mother Earth and Father God.*

The secret is there to discover, and it's time we become the nation of our declaration. And here is how we do it.

Petra, Jordan

The ship's bell of the "Columba" Santa Marie. One if the three ships the Vatican sent accrued the sea to take over those living for thousand of years in our Western Hemisphere.

The Cuban Capital building. Congress sits there. Built like ours but bigger. Built before Castro

The American Columba. That is before the creation of the third party federal reserve in 1913. We then became the new army of the old Roman Empire. Uncle Sam became our theme. And war for third party profit became the message of our nation.

This cubby-hole is inside the temple of Seti-Abydos Egypt. I am inside Diing my kundalini while exploring the site.

The eternal Cuban flame of Che. The flame being a Zoroastrians symbol. Older then Jesus. By the way they do let you take pictures at the Che museum.

A "holy man" in clay form. Pinocchio?

Primrose Hill. London. Where I sent into the wind some of the 20 earth elements ashes Of Barron. I was Telling the gathering those 20 elements go to earth. The 7 remaining elements go back to the matrix of existence. This game ends when our consciousness rejoins god. The circle in the picture says in Welch he who speak here speaks truth to power. I did not know that then when we had the gathering. It was pointed out to me after.

Me at the wailing wall Jerusalem.
Where I put some of my sons ashes.

Me being baptized in the Jordan river.
And yes Barron's ashes came and got wet with me.

Guest of Israel at the UN learning and meeting the creator of the Iron dome. The system that secured Israel's air waves.

Black Jesus. Portobello New Granada. Today called Panama. This was the statute of Jesus the slaves walked by on their way to enforced labor and death. The Vatican soldiers called conquistadors told the slaves this black Jesus would take care of them in the next Life. But for Jesus to do this they just work for them now.

Me in Petra Jordan riding the horses on the way to the historic rock fort we call Petra in Jordan.

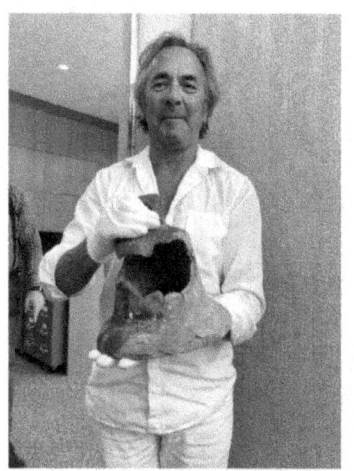

Me holding the Santa Marie bell.

The Mary of Guadalupe. The saint who got the Vatican's terrorists we call Spanish soldiers across the sea. Lol at the picture upside down and it appears to be corn. The food the killing visitors and slaves would use as their carbohydrate staple in their diet.

Me with the head soldier of Jordan.
Soldiers without them killing you for me or me
for you there would be no war.

Egyptian statue so old that biblical time had
not begun. From the area we call Luxor.

Barron and I riding in Memphis Egypt. Got into an argument
with Egyptian police. They told me to wear a shirt or else.
I said I am wearing a shirt. The shirt god and Mother Earth gave me.

Part Two
The Meta-Physical World System.

The Meta-Physical Game Running our Lives

The Meta-Physical World Order

Who are we?

Are we about to become an extinct species of human because we now failed to listen to nature's true call? A call led by the sounds and energies of natural systems collapsing due to sheer ignorance, the constant worship of money and greed as our god, while Mother Nature continues to change, to evolve and transform?

I see that could happen in my spiritual un-controlled dreams.

So, what can we do?

We need to understand the governments that have existed over time and what we need to do to create a government for the people and by the people and of the people, so we can survive and thrive as a species here and now on earth. Our consciousness playpen.

Government from beyond. Beyond our physical limitations.

I believe when we were created as angels, just not beast by God, with our body from Mother Earth, we were given the ability to govern our collective consciousness. The community of mankind. Not just a tribe and its ruler, or the big bully, physical bully of the community. This is a growing process. One that we learn from our past mistakes.

When do we commit to live as well as learn the Universal truths of both physical and spiritual laws?

When we go back to what is actually a matrix of energy. This is where we go when we leave our physical body and await our turn back on earth, or elsewhere, to be the very matter of spiritual fact.

We come back to earth, and we fall into the body, growing in our earth mother's womb. We awake in life, and we cry because we do not know where we are. We watch our parents and their friends and family make idiot facial expressions, trying to make us laugh. We cry and say, what is this? We forgot why we were here.

We grow physically, but we are brainwashed to forget the spiritual qualities. We fall into the living line of the current controlling system of education, religion, and economic game the few people who own and control our media play on us.

A paradigm that produces with intent, fears, and then hate, because we do not understand in our physical living form. We are all one. Time to shift this paradigm. Are we ready to be real pacifists? We want peace and we will be the first to get it.

In today's world, we become the beast of burdens. We serve those who control the necessities of our world. Necessities that must be owned and controlled by the real community of mankind.

We forgot we were coming back to share our awakening that we discovered when we were nothing but energy living in the matrix of existence. Really, what is God's mind?

The purpose of a government is to provide for the health and welfare, as well as the safety, for all its living form.

So now, how do we live and share life?

The problem with physical life, is to get physical energy, you must feed off other life. You kill both animals and plants to eat. We make up a social order and we then go kill to stay alive. Plants we can propagate. Animals we can propagate, but we do not recognize that all life has a consciousness. And this is the caste system of physical life. It is what the Hindus' knew.

Here is where the current living mankind, who call themselves Hindus' went wrong. Or how I was shown the spiritual vision from beyond.

They accepted the wrong caste system of fellow man. If you are aware something is wrong, it may not affect you, but if it affects other's way of life, I believe you have a duty to make people aware that it is wrong. But, then again, all religions of man-made gods do this in their own way. And I believe it is wrong.

Government is a spiritual contract between our consciousness that when we incarnate to date, we have allowed physical fears created by mankind to rule, take back our purpose in life. It is to be served and to serve fellow man. It is not a hell where we serve those who control our physical currency that we accept to work and live here on earth.

So, as I take us all down memory lane let's reboot the American experiment and where we fell off our mankind path forgetting:

- Earth does change,
- We must as a meta/physical consciousness adapt to these changes and
- We need a 21st century government by, of, and for the people to provide life, liberty and the ability to pursue happiness for All of us.

We must become the beacon of light showing all we represent God's love of fellow beings to the best of our current awareness and ability.

The Meta-Physical World

What is this? Let's go slow and let me try to open the passages in your mind so you can all see what I see. If we all close our minds to lies and fears, and just let the flow of breath take us over, my friends, you will for sure see where we all come from. Let's go there together.

Culture is the answer? Music is the vibration that can and does bring in change, or keep you the same. Music controls your thoughts.

> "The Word"
> "Stand"
> "Tears in Heaven"

Those are songs that meant so much in my life. And those last three words in my life bring to mind another great tune.

And, I am looking for someone to share that song in my life with, still. Maybe she has already appeared.

All a game. Two souls looking in the night to find the light and share their hearts together in happiness. Waiting for that kiss to wake up in your land of enchantment. All along our watchtower of consciousness, viewing how we deal with our lives.

But we are here on earth to live life. So, let me continue.

> *"Life, life tell it like it is. You do not have to die before you live."* --Sly and the Family Stone

What is life?

Life is physical and spiritual. Straight up. The twin towers of existence.

We concentrate on our sciences. We live off our technology. But both are the physical part of life.

Science teaches or explains nature's physical rules. Science is all theories and definitions. Explains what we presently accept as physical truths. But you can change the arc of physical realities. Remember, dimensions have time in space. Thoughts have no time and no space. And thoughts can move mountains and bring them to the sea.

Human spirit as well as consciousness can not, I repeat, cannot be defined by science. Human spirit is metaphysical. Why? Because human spirit is free will, not bound by the limits of time or space. We need a moral order to control, as well as encourage Free Will. Science, and its tools of technology, can not define what is a just society. Only our hearts can.

Part one was mostly all about our physical life. The "machine" that our individual consciousness lives in. What we need to know to survive. As an individual and a member of a tribe of a species we call humans.

But we did go over the creation and how our consciousness leaving God to become God, created our world with a big bank of thoughts and visual vibrational experiences that came to life. Life locked into a physical body, which controlled our thoughts and created new desires.

Like all animals, and for that matter, all living life, we need to get energy to use our body machine. We get this energy from eating physical forms of life, or drink liquids, which are enriched with the essential elements that keeps us keeping on.

Truth: we are a physical group of beasts. Humans consume other life, move the earth when possible, and do what's needed to survive. We build homes, communities, look for food, grow food, live by water.
Life is a gift. We get to experience physical sensations like all other creations.

But there is more; humans did not incarnate here on earth to be just beasts, or at least I believe so. We came to Earth to live amongst the beasts who exist as angels, so all life can enjoy the balanced planet. We walk in our body form.

Our consciousness in this body has three gifts other life Earth forms do not have. One, we can communicate individually our wants and needs with spirit. Two, we can interpret and improvise the messages we receive. Three, we can and do implement decisions our awareness from beyond this life shared with our physical brain.

Remember, the word genius in Latin, translated to English, means in touch with spirit. We are here to build a culture that can survive and thrive both individually and collectively. But to do so, we need to understand the game of creation, and why we incarnated to live this life. And yes, we have a choice.

We have rules that control what we do as individuals and members of different communities. But who makes up these rules. And why do we believe them to be true. Who are these rules for?

What century were these rules made in? And for whom were they made, and why? And most importantly, why do we believe them to be true? And then act and make them come true. What are we doing?

We say we want a just government to oversee us? Really? No, we want a just government to fulfill their obligations of servicing the people they represent. The government works for us. We do not work for the government.

This section was written over the course of my time running for the US Senate in 2016, and this year Congress, here in Florida. I wanted to serve the people. I want to light the fire in our bellies, so no one has to die from fear and uncertainty in a world that preys on each other. We are from the same source and that must be taught and retaught and just put into our DNA minds.

You are either a conservative or a liberal; that is what the mind thought control police put in our heads. That's all you are now allowed to be. Just like when you are born - you are your parent's religion as well as the child owned by the nation you were born in. You are a number under this system.

I believe you are not a number, and this game of labeling must go. How do we get rid of this system?

Broaden the boundaries. Understand the symbols of ownership and control of your mind. Learn the sacred meaning of the words in play which control your thoughts.

Let's examine culture and fashion as well as just government and conservative government.

Culture: It has been said that culture is conservative because it retains all that lasts the test of time, that it has "spiritual" value. And culture, by that definition, is for elitists, as only those few societies anointed commercially accepted as such few can be given the public gift of being considered timeless, and therefore of unique value.

Fashion is what the public today believes is new but does not have that test of time as proof that it is culture. Because culture requires the time factor to create the spiritual value of man-made controls over your mind.

Spirit is personal and communal. Spirit is your relationship with higher power. And this relationship is all about love and service to one another.

Culture can never be purely conservative because the essence of culture is the never-ending quest to discover the truth in an ever-changing world. New winds, new seas, new ground make our world on earth subject to change and that change creates the culture that helps society unite and get by each and every day.

We need a new culture for the 21st century. That is what spirit keeps showing me in my head. Just like the songwriters and script writers and fashion designers, as well as athletes, who became great spirit speakers, and these few know how to listen. I was not given a choice. I fought it off and lost. Spirit has won, and here is what they say, and what they show me to be true.

We need to find the way to create the new paradigm. And that paradigm will be based on either a just government for the few, the way we are currently heading, or a government for all the visions I see in my head. So folks, here we go!

So, let's lose the term liberal. It means anti-conservative. A conservative is one who lives a lie. Remember the song, *"A well respected man"*? Listen to it.

A conservative does not understand the winds of change; Wants everything to stay the same, so she/he, the conservative, can play their game knowing the land mines ahead. A lie to keep you believing that the world has not changed to keep only these few in power in control of you, the masses. The masses, the sheep people.

Culture on the other hand is the never-ending search for absolute creations. It is never pure because culture includes philosophy to get a just society. A just society is about social needs and these needs change with time. Our US Declaration of Independence of 1776 had values when we became the first nation in the world of our current written history to claim we are a nation. Those words were: "Life liberty and the pursuit of happiness."

Question; who was the "we" back in the days of the Declaration and the institution of the Constitution.

Our three promises to the creator of everything that we would be a nation without king or pope, but one for the people. And in those days, our founding fathers were not quite sure how to include everyone, because our world taught you that not all humans were people. We have moved on since then and own up to the fact that we were wrong.

Today we live in a mass democracy. One of quantity. Not one of quality. The game of mankind is to live life and to discover this physical life is temporary. But the essence of you, your soul is eternal.

We need to discover the eternal truth and beauty of existence. Not just the quantity of having a big possession-filled life. And a great teacher will help guide you to the path where you make your life eternal. Not just a moment in physical time. Remember, only physical life has time and space. So, who are we? And where do our Governments come from?

Creation of the Western Hemisphere's New/Old Order

In 1492, there were three culture-types of religious governments outside the natives who lived there then. Religion being the government. Conservative views were the culture of the lands.

1. Chinese

2. Vatican

3. Islamic

And we here in the US are the creation of thoughts from the Age of Reason and Enlightenment. The new world order of spiritual awareness as the world opened up from the inventions shared by the Chinese with Euro-Vatican controlled government.

The United States of America: Did you ever ask yourself where America came from? The name?

Well, even though this knowledge is now secret, the Chinese kept track of their story. Their history. So, we can dig away the dirt of Vatican-planned ignorance, and discover the pearls of our birth were our Euro and Chinese cultures, intersected around the middle east called the Silk Road.

China is not just a nation, but a civilization. What today I call a mass civilization. You do what the masses do. This is ingrained in their DNA. We know it as Confucius thought.

The rules of the Chinese Empire Order became a caste system of order and control. Order, to control Free Thought. You want Free Thought in this land? Good luck! The land is controlled as if they are human bees. The queen is the boss, and they all share the knowledge of their community.

Even Mao had to return to Confucius after he did everything to wipe it from the Chinese people's minds. This was after his dream of a country based on equality----a true communist state----while not understanding the real meaning of equality.

Communism, as we live it, is nothing short of a dictatorship-run economy. The few own and control the masses by owning and distributing the currency of the people.

We here in the US have a problem because our currency is distributed by a third-party cartel called the Federal Reserve. it is not federal nor a reserve. It must go, and I will get you there.

Those that own the distribution of the people's currency own the people.

The Chinese people wanted Confucius' back, under Mao. They got it with a new twist. A 21st Century rules of order and control design to make the Chinese civilization the dominant one of Mother Earth. Respect of your elders is one of their main themes. That is why the government has elders running their game.

Their economy is based on quantity. Not quality. The way to stop them is easy - cut them out. Forget about trying to make them just like us. They follow science and love technology. But only their way. Not a free will way. Not one that will grow. Just one that remains the same.

But do we here in the US? Think about it as I finish my story.

In 1421 the Chinese controlled the seas. They had the biggest Navy. And the Navy was boss.

The Chinese sent their ships to Europe. The goal was to awe the people of Europe to fall in love with the Emperor and his civilization.

They gave their knowledge, written in encyclopedias, to the people of the land we today call Italy. The rulers of a few city states. All controlled by merchants in business with the Vatican. Corrupt is too kind of a word to describe the Vatican 100 years before Martin Luther. The man who dared to tell the church you are an organization that lies and steals and covets others' property. You kill and maim. You are not what you say you are. The man was brave. I love his energy.

Freedom is when you learn you have nothing to lose. Time to be free, my friends. You do not die. There is no end. Learn this truth and the clowns who own this current system will disappear. They know the truth.

There were no books for the masses in 1421. Not even magazines or trash papers. No gossip. You went to Vatican questioning, the Inquisition, if you were found outside holding a public meeting. That is where the concept of conspiracy was created. A conspiracy to learn the truth. And today, with H. Clinton and D. Trump, to name only two, in control of the two-party political US system, you have to wonder what have we learned?

Truth will come out. It lives in the winds of the matrix and will appear. In fact, they could not read back then. The game was to keep the masses barefoot and ignorant. There was one book. It is called the bible; translated into English, it means the book.

It was written in Hebrew, Latin, Greek and a few other languages of limited use. This was about to change, and this change would turn the world over into our current living space.

But history shows things change, and the dark ages of Europe were about to get a shock wave. When times are a-changing, those in power do not read the falling leaves. They let the awareness become more dirt on the passage of time. They think they are too big to fall. Even Goliath fell.

We do not understand that we are both physical and spiritual. When human consciousness requires change, it will get it. And in this era, the desire of humans in Europe was fed by the printing press. The Chinese had in their Encyclopedia. It took time, but our Euro world changed.

The printing press changed our world. It opened up knowledge. Books of older times, before the creation of the Vatican, and their boys club of thought police, were copied and sold outside Europe. Knowledge became the new Game of the intellectual people prepared to die so they could learn in Europe. And so did the desire to live a life of quality. Discovering the true meaning.

Trade became the game of the few who had money to invest. It did not happen overnight. But the seeds of change were watered when the Ottoman Turks took over Constantinople, in 1453.

The Elite of the Vatican and their merchants and bankers lost their Far East water passage, and the Turks were now in control of the Mediterranean, as well as the water passages to the Indian Ocean.

A few who studied the Chinese Encyclopedia delivered by the Chinese to wow the West into submission, discovered maps of the world. These maps were hand copied, and then machine copied.

One of the few who copied these maps did so for the Vatican. His name as we are told was Amerigo Vespucci. Food for your thoughts; what does this name really mean. And who created this map and published it. The Vatican?

Amerigo is a Latin word that comes from a Germán name. Remember, the Vatican controlled the region we today call Germany, then and there. It was the Holy Roman Empire. The one that Hitler calls the First Reich. The second Reich of 1870, was English Victoria's grandson's the Kaiser's new nation, called Germany. The one that said Germans were a unique and special race. And yes, the royalty of England since 1713 had German blood and a German name. It gets crazy when you see how dumb we always were.

The word, a name is Emmerick. The name Emmerick means two thoughts. Rick is power. And E (A)Mer is work, labor. Meaning? The new world, through work, and ruling order, would be the purgatory for the masses that this new world will house to fill the ruling orders of the Vatican and merchants. Who were the merchants? The Italians of the city states of what today is Northern and Central Italy.

Vespucci is two words.. two. Ves is vessel. Pucchi is the family that controlled Florence and the Vatican. See their connections to the Medici family of the Italian city states. We are told a Germán copied the maps of the explorer we call Amerigo Vespucci. But if you believe the stories of the new world, the Pacific coast was not yet discovered—and yet it appears on this map--All lies to make you believe that the Americas' was a new world. It was not. Chinese and other Asian races settled here thousands of earth centuries ago. And in the South, they lived in slavery. Working and slaving for the platinum metals of gold and silver.

History is so important to know. The truth is so important to unravel. Why? Because the history creates the paradigm of those in control, so when we are young, we believe this is the way it was meant to be. When you learn it is the same game played by the few who know the rules of the matrix of creation, you realize how the masses of mankind have been played.

So, follow this truth. Mankind's story. Not the Latin story of the Vatican. The lies, by language, we today allow this crooked crew to rule the lands and divide society. A language the Vatican does not use as part of their brainwashing substance of controlled thoughts.

Incas were Chinese DNA. And the word Peru is Chinese. It means mist. And the Pacific coast of Peru is dry, with mist as its rain. It is the land of Nazca lines. I saw them in person, and it changed my life. I realized there was so much more.

So now named the 'Americas', the Vatican, with their conquistadors of the new 1400's Catholic nations, Spain and Portugal, created their new world order. Remember, if you were not Catholic you were tossed from these Euro lands. The game to remove you was called the Inquisition. Property was confiscated and no retribution was ever made.

Now, the Vatican game was to make the new world the utopia of the Vatican. This is exactly what Thomas More wrote about. The Vatican and their chosen few controlled the life style of these western hemisphere lands. No free will, like Jesus taught. No, there were only rules of Vatican order and control. Man-made Christ, the anti-Jesus in reality, was running their controlled spiritual show.

Also, please note that only a European born outside the new world, regardless of parents, could be a governor of these new world territories. And the homeland and their lifestyles of Catholic control was the ruling order. The Vatican game was for their land rulers not to have this new world as their own sacred space of birth. The allegiance had to be Vatican thought controlled European first.

The coast of Northeast America was different; it was run by networks of communities all married to Mother Earth. To nature. The people of the north's coast, and areas serviced by the rivers that flowed from the Atlantic to the Mississippi, lived life to enjoy and create. A life of quality. Not quantity for the few. These were the Indian tribes of North America. But that game would soon change. The English, the anti- Vatican, got their act together after they threw out the Catholic Church.

The French, still Vatican controlled, got their act together after the thirty-year war of 1648. They created the Euro lifestyles of North America inside the continent. The wars then were fought for control of the seas and the internal water ways. The French for the Vatican and the UK for the WASPs. The French just called their new world France. They had an absolute king. The British, with their Dutch and soon-to-be Germán king, created lands and lords all swearing allegiance to the King and the constitutional parliament of England, soon to be renamed the United Kingdom. A parliament of men called Lords who owned the land.

Our US nation was originally created as independent colonies, swearing allegiance to the motherland. Basically, colonies to feed England and Europe with the trade of product, not gold nor silver of the new world. Our northern indigenous tribes did not roll over like the southern tribes did. These tribes had order. Networks. Not Hierarchies. Where the new boss was not yet the same as the old boss

Even though the British won control with their guns, and by inflicting disease on the people of the land, the thoughts of those people are embedded in our creation as a nation. So are the principles of the Age of Reason, as well as Enlightenment. A federation not a central government of ownership and control. An essence way of life. Jesus, in fact, not Christ. Jesus, my friends is the anti-thought of Christ. The higher law is love not control. Wisdom that was buried; but now let's dig it up. So, let's continue digging it up.

Remember, wisdom grows, and then knowledge has no end. What we as a nation in the 1700's, in physical terms, worked for the agriculture and burgeoning Industrial Age. Our government was created for that world. Not this world. But the principles of people first must remain in this changing world.

At this time, capitalism did not exist as a word. Our land was based on Indian Wisdom of Mother Earth. Plus, Adam Smith's book on the Wealth of a Nation. The wealth is the people.

According to the Oxford Dictionary, the term "Capitalism" was first used by novelist William Makepeace Thackeray in his novel, *Newcomes*, in 1854.

The number one book in the 1770's was "Common Sense". Something our current mass democracy lost in the translation.

We need common sense to rule our land. We need to continue to grow. Spiritual growth.

We need to cultivate our souls. We need to study the metaphysical lessons of history we are given as truth.

We need to dissect what we are taught to understand - what lies beneath the surface of our taught history to become the humans we are capable of becoming.

Islam.

Why created? The ruling order of the Eastern Mediterranean in the year 622 was in disarray, and there was a gap which needed to be filled. Just tribes, and theft, and the Orthodox Greek Church overseeing absolute disorder, so they could stay in control.

By the way, the word Mediterranean is Latin, and means middle land. And you believe that this Vatican did not know what existed around our globe? You are taught they believed the world ended at the Atlantic. So how is the Mediterranean then the middle land? That is why this territory has been so important in world controlling thoughts and ideas. It is the middle ground of Earth.

The need was for its living people to become civilized to create a world without material first. The goal was social order to supervise building communities in and from the sand. The religion, as created, and taught by a man called Muhammad, around 622 AD was Islam.
He heard the Angel Gabriel.

Though we are told Muhammad could not write, the myth says he wrote down the sounds that became words and created what we are taught are the words of the Angel Gabriel. It says this was created in a dream. It was really the experiences he had with the metaphysical world. I believe he communicated with the energy from beyond called Gabriel.

The four Angels, which I refer to as the four winds, are Michael, Gabriel, Raphael and Uriel. Islam became the instrument of thought to create a world that would give the people a social order of their day to stop the wars of the tribes fighting for control of the Sinai Peninsula, as well as the land we call Mesopotamia.

Gabriel was the inspiration in the Abrahamic religions, which I call Hebrew, or today Jews, those from Judea, which was the name the Romans called those in revolt against their Roman tax schemes. Raphael is the Archangel, who appears and serves as God's messenger. It is Gabriel who appears to the Hebrew prophet, Daniel, to explain to Daniel, his visions.

The Islamic religion is based on the Hebrew traditions of how to have a just society. That is with one major exception. That exception is the religion created a social order to protect the people from other people who lived with this new religious tribe. This religion created a social order of rules and control for more than just God. It created the way of life, and justified war when the tribe was attacked, and prevented from doing their version of God's peaceful and loving work here on earth.

A world for the people of God to live in the desert of what we call the Middle East, in peace in the seventh century.

Things change, and this religion with its new social order went out and tried to conqueror their known world with this new social order. They went to war for the last twelve centuries with the rules and order of the Catholic Church and their Christ, not the son of God, but Christ the ruler of this Catholic self-proclaimed universe.

Today, the Christian world is still at Thought War with the Islamic world. In our world of alleged Christian traditions, in line with the Just God of the universe, we are taught to be afraid of the religious race that we call Muslims.

But what is a Muslim in the Middle East? A secular living human. A Muslim is a person of the city. An Arab is one from the desert regions, and a Moor is one from the agriculture world of North Africa.

Study history, recent history, and see how the Euro Christian nations have tried to own and control these lands. We have invaded and interfered non-stop in the local governments of these regions. Why? Two reasons. For the black gold called oil, and sea lanes trading routes to and from the Far East.

Today, with no higher purpose other than material possessions, we Euro descendants have declared in our minds that Islamization of our world is the greatest threat to our world order peace. Why? Because those in control will lose their material game. It will allow each community to compete just as we do in the Soccer/Futbol World Cup. May the best social order win, and then play again on an even playing field. Is that not the fair and correct thing to do?

What is the right way to live? What is the right way to have a real global society?

It is not allowing our nation to become the thieves of

the world for a business social order. Especially when they lie and say that this order is doing God's work.

Question? Whose God gave anyone the right to kill and maim? There is no Angel, just a man-made angel speaking for God, telling us to erase this population of people as our equals.

A simple thought for you all to answer to yourselves. Do we really believe that all Islam is trying to take over the US, or for that matter Europe?

Are there fundamentalists of Islam who wish to do away with our interpretation of the mass property society before God? The answer is yes. But are they a threat to our world more so then the order we are creating in our world? A world with no moral order. A world on the brink of creating a 21st century form of Fascism.

My friends, that is where we are heading, and the tea leaves are all around us to understand - what we are doing to ourselves by choice. We are now Mass Democracy.

Mass Democracy does not work. What is Mass Democracy?

Mass Democracy, really Mad Democracy, is when the businesses, for profit, both own and control the means of communicating, as well as educating our masses. Again, you have mass democracy. We are really out of our heart's control. We live in the mind that others create from this one game - thought control.

Now in the 1930's, this was a situation that we fought to save democracy. This is how the Nazi's took control. They put pac-man type business before the individual. The reason being that business, in their mind, at that time, was more important than the people.

Archangels: *Sidebar*

The other Super Archangels of that world have the following duties for God and communicate with those who choose to listen to their energies. Do I believe this? YES!

> **Archangel Michael:** Michael is the Earth's representative of the all-encompassing energy of strength of God. It is Michael whom one can talk with in that special metaphysical space and get the strength to defend your faith, as long as your faith is in line with the love of God.
>
> Michael is whom Constantine saw when he saw the white flag with the red cross and defeated his co-emperor in the early 4th century. After this unification of the Roman Empire, Constantine used Michael as his guide to create the true religion, which he called Catholic. A word that translates to English as *true*.
>
> The Hebrew meaning for Michael is "Who is like God". My point is all these earlier big three religions are based on the same

traditions and myths of the common man. These angels had no face, so Catholics created their god in man's image and called this God, Christ. They put a face on Love. When you have a face, you lose the imagination and you lose love, because the face becomes your controller. There is no face on the other religions. Just angels of energy that make things happen.

Archangel Raphael: Archangel Raphael is the supreme healer of the Angel world. He appears in the bible, as does Michael and Gabriel. His name means God heals in Hebrew. Raphael's chief role is to help you heal in all matters concerning your physical and spiritual health. In the Catholic world he is Saint Raphael, the patron of personal healing, physical travel and relationships amongst people. A real matchmaker.

Archangel Uriel: Archangel Uriel means God is my light. Uriel is usually the fourth angel of the Catholic points. Uriel is the angel who spreads the wisdom of God. Go to your special metaphysical space and ask for the wisdom of God, and the voice you may hear, if not God, is Uriel.

In the spiritual Angelic world of the Judeo-Christian-Islamic world, we can learn of four super angels. The angels who communicate with us for God, the ultimate creator of everything, and his son, the creator of our universe, the energy the Christians call Jesus the son of God, and whom the Islamic recognize as a super prophet.

All these religions are based on metaphysical communications. But this sacred knowledge is now secret knowledge. We are taught the physical world is all that matters, and here, in what we call the western world, the physical world is material. We live in the sin of mammon before we live with God. And that, my friends, is what needs to change, or we will become extinct, like all the beasts that controlled earth before us.

Before I leave the Islamic world, a quick study is in order of the way the nations with oil in the Arab Peninsula run themselves. Their religion is their ruling order. They are at war over their interpretation of what is the proper path back to their Prophet Muhammad, and his message from God.

The Shiites and the Sunnis. That is their own social disorder. God does not make rules. Man does. Man makes the rules to keep their unique vision of their interpretation of God as the only interpretation.

The lands with the ruling kingdoms, such as Saudi Arabia, Kuwait and UAE, have rules made to keep the people in line. They have a social order where everyone has health care. Everyone has education, and everyone gets a piece of the oil profits. But everyone must pay respect to their ruling order.

The other problem for the Christian world order is an Islamic can not borrow money with interest, as opposed to partnership. If you go into business with them, their religion as Jesus, the Islamic prophet, not

Christ, himself said, does not allow you to pay back an extra charge. You can get money and go into business, but you as a person and a society cannot borrow money and pay back the interest, if you as mankind do not have profit. Is that why Christians hate this religion? Because they will not incur personal debt and then become the slave for that debt? Think about it.

The Columba of the U.S. Colonies.

How do we change? Well, let's look what changes we made here in the US since our founding fathers created the living earth board game called the United States of America.

What is this document known as the Declaration of Independence, signed by our founding fathers of 1776, really all about? Why is our Capital called Washington, the District of Columbia? What is a Columba? What is the America of our founding fathers dream?

As you read earlier, the Vatican in the 1400's set up the development of the Americas, where minerals were found by others in the ground. As well as found the Fountain of Youth somewhere in today's Florida.

Their goal was to get the gold and silver and then create their paradise in this new world order. Get the conquistadors to come to the new world searching for their El-Dorado. Then the killing crew will stay, reproduce and serve the new ruling order of the Vatican. In fact, they said let's call it Latin America, so we declare these lands as ours, even though no one but us and with the Catholic Church hierarchy will speak the secret tongue of Latin. This was the game plan to set up and to have their Utopia, where they are served by everyone else.

Then with this gold and silver, the Catholic Church would create the society that they called the New World. They would own our consciousness because they never learned the lessons of King Midas. Inconsistent thoughts of ownership to control.

This new world was created by the key words Christopher Columbus. Not a man but a vision. A new paradigm of Catholic social order. Social control of the masses.

Columbus, as I wrote earlier, in English, translated back to Latin, refers to a Columba in Latin. A pigeon then that was a messenger who is put in flight as a carrier of a message. The three ships, which are called Santa Maria, Pinta and Nina, were the "pigeon" carriers of the message of Christopher. Christopher, in Latin translated to English, means the bearer of Christ.

The question then becomes which Christ? Whose Christ? The answer was the Catholic Church Christ. Not Jesus, but their ruling man-made God, Christ.

The face we see as Christopher Columbus is made up. There is no image made while he was alive. Neither painting nor sculpture of the man's living image. But there was a man who captained these ships.

In Spain, there are tales of the captain being called Pedro Scotto. The Spanish crowd got the crew and may have financed part of the trip. If they did finance it at all, they did it in partnership with the Catholic Church, and the Medici banking family of that era.

The Catholic Church government which we have been calling the Vatican, and so will continue that terminology, with their seafaring Iberian Peninsula of lands, which today we call Spain and Portugal, divided the ownership of the new world between those two Iberian nations. The peninsula the Romans called Hispania, are the lands we know as Haiti and the Dominican Republic. Portugal got the East, and Spain got the West. The dividing point is the Canary Islands.

Later, Holland, France and England got involved in exploration and trade of precious items, which Europe wanted and needed. The three of them fought over who would control the North American masses. The English won this battle in the 1700's. In 1688, the English parliament hired William of Orange, part of Holland, and King James' daughter, Mary, to be the King and Queen, but their children could not inherit the throne. That was Statutory - saved for Anne, the last living daughter of James the Second, the Catholic, who the Brits got rid of. Then followed the German Dynasty, that to this day still fronts the Kingdom. Can't beat them or hire them. And with this victory came their ruling social order.

The Declaration of Independence is the only time man, as a group, created a country. It is a declaration of their new paradigm. A land of equals, saying we will create a land of life and liberty for all that we recognize as full human. And this land will be the place where all can pursue happiness without kingdom or pope. That was our message. That was our new nation's Columba. And that is the metaphysical reason that we chose the district that houses our capitol as the District of Columba, written in English as Columbia, to let those in the know of the sacred knowledge, that that is our message.

A land where we will try to become the one where all can have life with liberty and pursue happiness.

That is under our rule. Our dream that we sold to the world. A dream the world believes - and I believe we can do it. Hence this book.

We started our land as a federation. A land where there was no hierarchy of rule. It was a federation. In essence, 13 networks called states, agreeing to work together as equals, and protect their people from invasion of others. The fourteenth was Vermont, but they were Catholic and not yet invited into this Northern Euro rule. They were their own country from 1777-1791, when Vermont joined the Union as state 14. But the Federation had a really big problem. No customers. Just themselves looking to come and take what they could. And why that problem?

The problem was that there was no one central authoritative voice, a voice that had control of the organization and could make commitments that others could rely on when promises are made, and solutions are needed.

In business, an open market of equals does not build a land that outsiders will invest in for their personal profit. So, 13 years after the Declaration, we created a Federal Government to provide the health welfare and safety of its people, and lesser, who were not yet qualified to be full citizens.

It is important to remember that our current government was created to protect the masses-- originally a nation of agriculture-- as well as encourage the development of industry and trade with the European world that existed at that time. The north would copy England soon and become the home of the new technology of the industrial revolution. The south would stay agrarian.

Our new world was now a world that was no longer ruled by the Catholic Church exclusively. As Europe industrialized, the religions of the region changed. There was now a competing religion. One that had no spiritual backbone. It was all about living in the physical world. It was about the here and now. It is what we call the Protestant religions. No Hierarchy, each person discovered their own version of Christ.

When you stop living off the land you forget the wonders as well as living lessons of nature. You also lose the metaphysical spirit of life in the urban jungle. Today, we as a nation have lost the wonders of nature and this must change, or earth will change, and we go as a species into the delete category. We lost the spirit side of life. We are animals who live and die to accumulate everything we do not need but are brainwashed to want at the cost of our soul.

We have become an industrialized nation that worships technologic advances, which in turn enslave us even more. Truth. And science, we do not have the money to invest in creating. We have the money to lie and bribe those to say this is the need, there is nothing better than what we own already. Luckily, there are many alive who are outlaws from injustice, and still pursue the truth for consciousness.

When created, as I said previously, we were supposed to be the land without kingdom or pope,--- the 1788/89 constitution, BUT Big WASP brothers who controlled the masses created a three-branch government of equal branches for them, with the dream for everyone else that this land could be for everyone. All with checks and balances to stop our land from becoming one big thought-controlled hierarchy, or in reality a government that could legally tie up and stop change.

And this thought control US of the 18th century is still in control. WE actually have people who say the constitution is sacred and can not be interpreted for the living citizens of the 21st century.

The essence is for all, the rulers and legislatures are for the few. The government must be returned to the essences. It can be done. Let's do it.

We need to change this paradigm. Our 21st Century laws must be broken up, or we will become slaves to the few who will live off our work energy until earth gets rid of us.

Darwin is wrong, as we are taught. We are taught only the strongest survive. That is not true. Follow the light. Choose God as our friend and father for life. Let God inspire, as God did say to go create, but never said to kill and maim. We must stop killing and maiming mother earth, or we will have nothing left to fix or conserve.

Only the wisest survive, and the wise do see and the wise are in contact with spirit, who wants all of us to survive and live life in this physical heaven earth was meant to be.

Some questions for all of us. Who pulls our strings? Who makes us act? Who writes the play of our lives? The answers, I believe, are the following.

The directors of the play, which I call life, are the spirits of the matrix, living and breathing thoughts and ideas down our throats like a coach playing offense and defense too, in the football games we watch and love in our current world order of amusement. Men wearing new gladiator suits beating each other up to get a pigskin across a goal line by foot both on the ground or in the air.

<u>The United States of America.</u>

Mass Democracy

<u>In the year 2020. We have two paths. One is into the light, or two, to stay in our darkness. The shadows that others throw on us to keep us working and slaving for the few, as they live off you.</u>

<u>Questions we ask and never get an answer. We get a new crisis that makes us lose our thoughts. We get new fears. Ever ask why the mass shootings in our land make news for a few days and then go away?</u>

Let's send this living nightmare to the graveyard. Let's become the greatest nation ever. Where every man and woman can be the King and Queen of their dreams, as there is enough for everyone.

We need to begin this section letting you know I will be sharing with you my awareness to what the few are doing to us. I will share this vision with you. I will share with you my own sacred knowledge behind the definitions of words, which have become symbols to our current society. Knowledge that is hidden from all of us so we conform and let others own and control our breathing hours here on earth.

What is freedom? What is the cost of Freedom? When do you fight for your freedom? Is it only when you have nothing else to lose? What are you afraid to lose? Do you want to live your life on your knees? Begging and just saying please? Or live your life with the confidence to know you were not made to be someone's number?

You are unique, special and extraordinary and you must protect yourself as well as others. Why? Because we all deserve life with just liberty and the ability when we are ready to pursue our dreams.

I believe freedom is where you can live your life with a just government that represents both you the individual and we, the community. Not statutes of laws, but understanding and equitable relief for the living while they are living.

In case of doubt, the community must always come first and foremost. When the health and welfare of the community is placed in imminent harm or danger, we must protect the community.

When society doing business is the danger and the people want the
behavior to end, then the test to figure out or move, must be the following: what does the conduct do to the individual business and to the whole of our society? It is a scale of morality that we must weigh. Society must win.

Again, the legal system must be based on equity, not **statutes,** which **prescribe** behavior based on the past and without considering the change of circumstances that happens in physical life. Equitable relief is the key.

When you study the real history of mankind in community form you will learn that civilizations fail not because they have to, but because the ruling elite did not pay attention to the changes in our consciousness as a species, due to the change of circumstances of life itself. Or the elite went out of

their way to protect their own individual interest at the expense of the
whole. Remember the phrase, "let them eat cake"? Well, the French did, and so started the French revolution of the 1780's and 90's.

What is Life in a metaphysical world?

We live in a meta/physical world. It is hidden from we, the masses. Intentionally, I must add. The goal, from here on out, is to open our eyes so we can say we are mad as hell and we are not going to take it anymore. The game now is to start the path back to reality for all living in the meta/physical world not just the material world.

Life in the metaphysical world to begin with: It is one where possessions are not **the most important** first and foremost. What the Bible refers to as mammon. You cannot have two goals of aspirations in life. Your choice. Is it to live first with God, or to live with possessions first. Not both. And you can have God and possessions but to kill and maim and live a life on your knees asking for forgiveness or begging for help? Wrong life.

The goal of life is to live the life as an angel to the best of your abilities. It is intuitive. We have the tools. And the elders of each society should be the coach to help the young understand the game of physical and mental life. How to use your tools not just react to your urges?

Education is key. Education today has become all about possessions. Spiritual life has gone **bye bye**. We need to educate all about what it is like to be a person in touch with both spirit and physical nature. Not just your big boy toys of possessions and what? Honor your Mother earth and Father God. Do not destroy earth so you can live without regards to other humans, as well as all living matter.

When the concept of our current democracy was created in the Age of Enlightenment, the goal was to copy Athens and spread it from there. Thanks to the Arabs, the books of Socrates, Plato and Aristotle were rediscovered. The Vatican's attempt to hide the universal truths by burning books and controlling knowledge of the world before, the Vatican failed.

Plus, the history of man's physical creation is buried in the sands of earth's time. When we look, we shall discover the pieces of man's earlier times here on earth. We just need to be willing to learn, as we become aware of the Columba of those pieces.

Yes, you read right. The Catholic Church, in its past, starting in 392AD, in the city of Alexandria, used to burn the books that taught reason. Philosophy was banned, as it made you question hierarchies that controlled your life. Then, the Jesuits, the thought control police force of the Vatican, started banning books because they opened your minds. The Jesuits knew the truth, but you were not allowed to know it, as you were not ready, they claimed.

But in this age of 1700's, Reason, not just Democracy was their goal. Democracy was their growing concept, no borders, to live on earth with a spiritual side to your life. What Jesus, the man, taught, and what man-made Catholic Christ denied.

Yet, we have many who say why make change. Change a document that was for WASP men on the most part, who owned property when written. A document that worked to give the vote to the allowed whites only for a legislative position.

Let's go to the here and now.

We are a meta/physical consciousness. Spiritual and physical combined. This book explains this universal truth to you.

The problem with the spiritual side of our existence today, is we live in the age of science and its sister technology. In this world, ghosts and spirits do not exist. But yet Science can not physically explain with a complete understanding how the human being reasons and moves. We take polls, and guess what? They are not accurate. We try to fix the results, and that does not work, too.

Why? Because science of documented physical proof can never quantify the instincts that make conscious man change patterns. The desires of man, the virtues and values are a changing vibration.

Science and technology owned privately by the few, have become what rules our current world. And these devices have helped to make this new world order.

This is the beginning of what I now call Mass Democracy. Those who have the right possessions that society teaches you one must have are the celebrities, and the only ones to be worthy of respect. Except, the new Gods are the ones who own the technology, and their new political royal courts of jesters acting like fools.

Follow as we get right into what we now are. What we have become.

Science is ruled by a fixed paradigm that requires data that becomes concrete proof. Definitions are then created that are black and white. This black and white is the law of physical thought. Just straight lines. Lines that go against the circle of life. We live a life of seasons that changes our outlook each and every day. But we want guarantees, so we sell straight lines of thoughts.

Our schools no longer teach the how, what, or why. We teach it just as it is. And we divide the human race into divisions caused by fears with the intent to divide our culture. Schools of thoughts with 1) No humanities. 2) No art. 3) No culture.

This leads me to define culture. What is culture? Culture is what creates a human civilization. A civilization that grows. Not one of vampires controlling the zombies of Despotic Hierarchies of ownership and control, the Dark Ages.

When culture stops, so does the society. Globalization of science and technology should have opened up the sharing of culture and made us all better. I have spent my life learning and sharing cultures from all over the world

But...We have failed mankind of the future. How? Ask yourself is this the world you want your children and your children's children to grow up in?

Can we change?

Follow me. I say yes, but it ain't easy.

Here is the current failure.

What happened is unregulated mass business, and business for paper profits without any controls to stop vampire behavior has made us a nation without any morals. We are all about possessions.

We have made school education all about multiple choice.
There is no reason. Again, no morals. Nothing but how to make work to make money. And those who make it big following the leaders and doing what they are told become our celebrities and who we follow.

I made and worked with as many celebrities from the 70's as anyone still alive. Bold statement and true. I am disgusted by what I helped do to society. My book, *Gods, Gangsters and Honor,* is all about this truth.

These celebrities are no different than you, except you are convinced they are better than you. Truth is, many know they are not, and cannot live the lie. Which is why, instead of doing drugs and drink, the drugs and drink do them, and life ends quicker than it should.

Trumpism is America of today. Trumpism is more than the face of Donald Trump. Look at the choice that we had running against Trump. Nobodies? Meta/physical deficient lost souls. Just bricks in the wall of a very broken system of thoughts and controls. Zombies working for the International Monetary Fund (IMF), and here in the US, the Federal Reserve. Keeping paper profits and people in debt is the game of winning here in the US.

It is now the halfway point between Mass Democracy and Fascism. It was created by the living dance of both the Republican and Democratic parties. Both parties created a nation that responds to ads. Yes, ads. Telling you what to do and how to do it. Gives you choice without reason.

Trumpism is the end game of mass democracy, and it is also why our nation, here in the states, needs a 21st Century overhaul. Just as Thomas Jefferson said, each generation needs its own constitution.

Mass Democracy is what we have become. And fascism is a day away, because fascism feeds on the energy of the masses. Fascism has come to America through democracy. Big brother is lurking in our backyard. Trump is the leader of this new movement for the moment because of his celebrity-hood. He will be replaced. We either return to real democracy or we keep moving from Mass Democracy to fascism, and then the end game of despotism with mass violence.

What is Mass Democracy? How did this happen to us?

There is a vibration of thought that exists in all our minds. A vibration of fear. A vibration that gets us to act without morals and as beasts. Just act like all members of the animal kingdom. It is a chord in the piano of our thoughts, and when played, makes us lose our angel consciousness of humankind.

If fear is our culture, we have lost the game of life. We now are living in a box of man-made fears that are like needles in our imaginary beds of pain.

Culture is either mammon or spiritual. If spiritual, culture teaches you about the evolution of the human condition during the passage of time. Culture of spiritualism is based on wisdom. Culture of wisdom is song, dance, poetry, paintings, novels, philosophy, even theology, too. It is all the arts and the reinterpretations of history as mankind sees it when the story is written. In the present, not just living the past.

Lack of growing culture, you have a recipe for the current era's return to fascism. We no longer have values as the main pillars of society that go to the goodness and growth of human spirit. No, our values are all "I want what they have".

The pursuit of happiness is the key to our declaration of 1776 to the world, and our maker. It is where the human spirit was supposed to grow. Not where we create a land for the few to win and that controls our happiness with debt to a banking industry that only circulates our own paper currency. NEEDS TO STOP!

Please remember a banker by trade is a really an accountant job. It is not to gamble or invest your money. They are to protect your funds. Get it? No, you don't. We give them the energy to believe they are the masters of our universe. How? We are a very greedy lot.

Bankers. They do as their taught, and told. They are the well-paid slaves of the few who control the distribution of the currency that we use to sell our time or products we need or want to play the physical game of life.

Why are they given a position in life higher than the real heroes of our lives, our police and firemen. Those who work the emergency rooms and save lives. Not steal and trick you into buying what you do not need. Or get you to buy, so they, the bankers, can get out of their position of selling stocks or bonds as well as real property, too. Too often they held what you just bought.

While I am not a preacher, I do see things for what their intrinsic values are. Do our movements help the individual and the whole of society? Or just the individual? We need both, or we lose democracy.

So today our America in verse is the following world:

> *"A nation where people join the club, dress the same, say the same things, send their kids to school to learn the new golden rules, make money, not art. When you have the money you become king, and are worshiped by others who are taught by the media they need to grow up and be exactly like you. Same schools, same clubs, art of consumption, not food for thought. But food to*

keep you asleep at the wheel of life. We are a nation of sheep people now on auto pilot."

The media is not neutral. No, the media is the means by which the few gain control of our minds. The media even have us the watching public as members of the two clubs, known as the Democrat and Republican party. Today, both work for the same independent banking system that distributes our currency for a fee.

The bankers and the media and our big corporate executives, too, as well as our politicians, all dress the same. But no one sees them as the sales point for life interpretations to be sold on how we are America the great, and the rest of the world is beneath us. We are the masters of our universe.

The media networks, which have public persona, have the same boy and girl haircuts. They are diverse in skin color or sex just to have tokens. The media has become Stepford humans. No personalities, just repeat as we need. Even in sports, this is now going on. Emotion is the love that has been buried. Passion is left in our sinks. Truth, the media is helping us bury our love.

I ask you, is it over, or is it not?

These bankers forget they are one of us. These bankers who gamble our deposits, they call it investment, rob the public of their pensions and their hopes and dreams. But when we catch the thieves, we are told they are too big to fail, so we buy them out of the crimes they committed. We have socialized their losses and privatized their gains.

Hello, Mass Democracy. A land where the goal is to get you to believe that life is about enjoying yourselves, providing that is all you think about. To make this happen, we need a hierarchy that gets all the networks of communities to report in and tell others, they will make sure this elevates life and stays this way.

No longer the home of the free let alone the brave. We are politically correct, which means we lie to others as well as to ourselves. We do not have the nerve to question and make change. We live in the shadows cast on our bodies as the lights are now put out.

We are aware, but we bark, but then we go back and work to pay the bankers the monies we owe, calling them DEBTS for letting us live in this nation, once the greatest nation, we are taught, ever created. But today, the biggest living lie on the planet.

How did we get here? We did this. Without force and really choice. We followed the paper money. And money, as King and God, has ruined our souls.

And if you question this mass democracy, you are an outsider and will be displaced as the end game. The powers in control do not want others running around to wake us up from our sleeping beauty sleep. We need the kiss from God to live again. The breath of truth to fill our hearts and move our souls for the benefit of all earth.

But I must ask you, does God want us to be physically and individually separate and trying to become physical Gods anymore? What have we learned? Anything?

What is the original meaning of culture? It comes from two words. These words are cultura animi. The words together mean cultivation of the soul. An idea in all our big three monistic religions that mankind must elevate themselves by rising above their animal instincts and needs we spoke about.

You do not die, my friends. You just leave the playing field and return to the matrix. And yes, you become a spectator again. Rooting on those you played the game of life with, so they can have eternal peace and not live in purgatory trying to get back here and win the game of ownership and control.

I believe in absolute truth. That truth is eternal. And not external. What we see and experience, we create. We need our elders to teach the real end game of life here on earth. That game is to live in truth, doing what your heart says is right, day in and day out. Sharing the beauty of living, and not taking away the soul, so only the elite can prosper with mammon.

Naked truth.

One who lives as a slave to their desires, emotions, fears that become prejudices and loses the ability to use their intellect is not free, nor will ever be free. No, they are but a beast of this world.

When nothing has spiritual values, then meta life here on earth is over. We are now ready to become the pharaoh's new slaves. And remember the Egyptian priest who ran the game controlled the pharaoh. The Game is to control life here on earth with a celebrity, and your belief -by obeying the priest, your next life will be better.

Today's priests are the one-world banking system led by the IMF. In our land, the banking cartel that calls themselves the Federal Reserve. What a con; but the schools that control our thoughts, and the media that sends the message never question this game and how to make new rules that would apply to the 21st Century, not 1913, the year the game became our independent central bank. That Federal Reserve scam was the crime of the last century. The end of Jefferson's democracy.

Our founding fathers knew that the people of the nation must control their own currency. The founding fathers' sin is they did not deal with the economic realities of life. They left it out. The truth about a central bank is it must be owned by those who run the game. We the people, must be taught we run the game. In Monopoly, the game, we do. The banker is one of us. In life, we elevated these asses; donkeys who steal for the few as long as they get to eat a little too. Pinocchio's at work.

If we the people do not control our currency, then those who control it control you. To stay in control and stop people like me, they create the culture of Mass Democracy---

Where the threat of danger lives to become permanent aggression concealed beneath the taught thoughts of prosperity.

The game our system of control now plays. All one big game. Why do people lie?

Mass democracy requires Mass Mankind. Where both sexes believe the same thing. The pursuit of property, not happiness. It is a mindset. Really in truth, an absence of mind.

Now once you have mass man, and in our nation, it is republican or democratic values we are taught. We do not realize that the banks and their media separated us into these two categories. Us and them. But in the end, we are all the same, but we are not taught that spiritual truth any more. The banks say they are the neutral party.

The Vatican and its Holy Roman Empire, in 1648, created this game when Switzerland became a neutral land. A land so neutral that any thief could go and stash their stolen goods there. And so, you really believed Switzerland is neutral, the country's military protects the Vatican. Why? So, you think the nation is in business with God? Unreal.

This is the land that fenced all the stolen arts and treasures of the Jews who were being slaughtered by the grown choir boy named Hitler. The Vatican did nothing. Just let the game go on. And then started their propaganda and said we had nothing to do with the killing. Yet we are told they are God's representatives here on earth. So, God did not tell these few living in their material world to stop the deaths. God may run from this crew. Fraud is a crime in every just mind.

We here in the USA believe that it is our way or the highway. The others must adapt, and we live in a society that charges for every breath you take, every sip you drink, and every thought you can no longer have. Question this system again, you become an outsider.

Mass MAN is always right. Needs no further justification.

Now, to have Mass democracy of two parties working for the same banker's control, you must control the message. You must own the media.

When our nation was younger then today, we did not allow one party to own the media the way we do now. Newspapers, Radio and TV were not Big Business. They were independent.

Starting with Reagan, this changed. Media started becoming a hierarchy of thoughts, and therefore, control. No independent networks. Just mass ownership, with the mass message. Consume. Buy. Borrow. Be rich and affluent like these others who succeeded.

Mass media is the greatest training ground for birthing new demagogues. How? Well, the media feeds you trivia. It's all sensationalism. Really nothing of eternal growth substance.

The art of dialog has been reduced to slogans, all for propaganda. Tweeting is our school system. Not thoughts, just messages.

And Facebook has become the end game, where the consumer is the product. Endless game of mind control, where your independent thoughts are trolled, and messages are crafted, so you will go and buy.

Facebook, which was created by a few horny college entrepreneurs, college kids running their own fraternity social club, sold out to the bankers and is now just a mass democracy tool. And these heartless clones go around justifying their social crime. They stole your identity.

The Internet. If ever something should be open to all and administered by the government of the people, it is the Internet. We just do not have the brains to make it stay this way.

We hear net neutrality. That is not freedom of access. We need a public, free, wifi system. For all. I ran for Congress trying to teach the lie of net neutrality. Because I was not on Fox or CNN, I was not heard.

The Internet is the tool of Mass Democracy. It will help enslave us. We will become technology zombies. Watch it happen if we all sit and do nothing.

You get tired of this endless deluge of brain-numbing warfare on your mind, so you look for a leader to make it simple, and you stay stupid. We want it simple, and what can be simpler than Trump. He is the mass democracy hero for the moment, until those in control toss him and take absolute control of our minds and souls.

We crave stimulation of the empty mind kind. Trump is the perfect Nero (the last roman emperor of the

Julio-Claudian dynasty) for this game. All we do is look for a drug of some kind to numb us out to stay inside this insane system of thought control. Even the doctors will give you mood pills to numb you out so you behave, and not question the loss of life with values. No life in this mass game is all about accumulating possessions at the cost of your soul.

Think how many of you are on these mood pills. How many years are you on it? And what is your ability to relate with emotions or caring to the plight of fellow man. Where are you?

A true democracy is not based on our differences. No, a true democracy must be based on what makes us equals. That quality is the ability for each and every one of us, all over the planet, to elevate our souls. To live in eternal truth. To do what God commanded; go create a better world for all mankind. Understanding the balance nature must keep, so this playing field stays the way it is and allow us to have our consciousness live in these bodies that age and wear down.

Another rule of Mass Democracy is that if something is difficult to understand, then it is undemocratic. It is elitist, and not for the people. Mass Democracy rules are keep dumbed down and not think provocative thoughts. How many intellects are given space on the mass media hysteria channels? Think about that.

This rule is as old as society trying to be democratic. Even in Athens, of Socrates's day, Socrates was put to death for teaching his students to use reason and constantly question the ruling status quo. On his death, his last words are reported to have been.

"If I cannot teach people reason, then this world is not for me."

When movies became big business, the trick was to grab the audience. The big budget movies needed a financial return. I learned this game well when I was involved with movies. Big and small.

The big movies had to go to the lowest common denominator of society. That denominator is fear and hate. So, the movies became fear and hate. Not all, but the big budget ones sure did this game.

There are exceptions which I must share. You did have the family ones, which were all animated for the most part.

These animated movies dealt with spiritual values hidden inside stories. Movies like *Wall-E, Spirited Away* & *Coco* (a story of the metaphysical world) are great examples.

I write this here because we are not over as a race of higher consciousness. We just need to make sure we have spiritual values incorporated in our culture once again. Real soon. Or else…

To get a TV audience our newscasters exploit resentment. They promote fear, not love, not the one society of mankind. Never do you hear about what society did good today. No, you hear what went wrong, because we are programed to want to hear failures.

Watch the news and listen to the weather portion. If it's partly cloudy, is it not also partly sunny? Well, why tell us the dark when you can share first the light.

Society, here in the USA, likes to divide. There is more negative power in numbers if you learn to divide. There is love in uniting and the ultimate power of growth and real prosperity.

What our society has allowed to happen is the division of our society into a super group, and then the subcategories of the rest. Our political powers cater to this division instead of uniting all in one race of mankind.

At various political debates and rallies, while running for office, as well as my coming to terms with my son's idiot murder, I have repeatedly told the audience that we do not want to have just gay rights, or LGBT rights.

We have to have people's rights, and people have a right to do what they wish in their personal decisions on how they choose to lead their lives. The government has a duty to insure those rights.

I'm here to tell the people all of us have the same people rights. When you allow the powers to divide us, you, in the sub-category, have made yourselves in the minds of others a lesser race than the whole. We need to get back to respecting each other as equals. This starts in school.

Let's go to black-skinned African-Americans. This is a wrong division, too. First off, the black-skinned people in America are no more African-Americans than I am. If we believe the story of physical mankind evolution, as we are taught in our school system, we all came from one common ancestor named Lucy, who lived in the African continent. We all learn, then and there, we are one race. Our society must instill this truth to our children.

Second, and hear this truth. The blacks were sold by their families to the slave traders. The blacks in the western hemisphere have an issue with the Africans, as they were sold as merchandise. And this has not settled spiritually, let alone even discussed. And the kicker is, in 1453-1455 the Vatican, led by Pope Nicholas, created a papal bull which gave Catholics permission to buy these unwanted people.

So wrong, and so buried in our dirt. When we raise these dead truths, and throw out the lies, we will learn once and for all that this system of ownership and control, with permission from a god, to kill and maim does not work. We need a new system.

America is a land of division. We will fall, unless we try to unite and stand together as one people of our common land.

Case in point is the musician known as Drake. A black-skinned man of Canadian nationality. Why is he not referred to as an African-Canadian? Why? Because the Canadians have more common sense than we do, and will not let the few divide their country, as we did and still do.

Again, I must repeat, we are one race of many cultures. America does have a Black culture. It is based on family and building community. I know it. I have spent my life cultivating the arts of these communities throughout the USA in song and dance, plus the occasional movie.

The continent of Africa has many cultures. All different and not American, let alone Black American. I know this, as I have spent a good deal of my life time cultivating and promoting various musical artists from many nations of Africa. Each has their own unique and special way of sharing the love and ideas that are their spiritual side explaining love the way they feel it. Including not feeling it at all.

In the 80's I was named *"Black Music Manager of the Year."* I grew up with black athletes and performers, as well as producers in my home. I was lucky. I learned diversity real quick.

My life became Pop Culture. I experienced the division of our mankind when people started dividing the blacks from the whites in the media and elsewhere. Why? Power in numbers.

We represented a music label from Philadelphia, called Philadelphia International. They had many musical hits in the 70's. And I loved the owners of the label, Kenny Gamble and Leon Huff. I was so excited to finally be able to represent them legally. My father was their lawyer from their beginning.

I will never forget Kenny Gamble telling me that I cannot be the face of the business legal team because

I am white. Why? Because society was requiring him to hire blacks to be the face of the company. I asked him why? He said he was powerless.

I got mad, but I did tell him, there is your new song. It is discrimination in reverse. You can not tell people who they must associate with. You can help guide people to lose the fears we all have when we see something different from what we are used to seeing. Not fear, to become hate, and therefore controlled by those who can contain the fear they created. No acceptance and growth. Learn the many true cultures of mankind. Not the ones based on ignorance.

In the 80's, while I was managing black acts, MTV became the media. A song of images was now reduced to a video of one-dimensional thoughts. The words no longer let you reach your own conclusion, but the words became a movie of commercial control. A control it was.

MTV killed the arts of poetry and song. It helped create the world of gangster rap. How? Well, because cable was then underground, the black communities did not have it, and therefore MTV did not cater to a black audience. It would only play videos that their white and affluent audience would watch as POP. This is how Michael Jackson was created. Tons of money spent on marketing him as androgynous.

Just a neutral performer. Made him their meal ticket and helped destroy a man whom was not ready to be a God. My book *"Gods, Gangsters and Honour"* deals with this marketing of people to make them celebrities, so everyone can feed on them, and if the owners are lucky, they die from trying to be the manmade Gods they are not.

So, if you are marketing US black music before the Internet was created, how do you get it on white, or elite TV? Easy, go to the lowest common denominator. Hate and fear. Have the blacks act as beasts. The video-created gangster rap videos have opened up a culture of youth to gang violence and hate of others who were not "like" them.

Video games knew this culture in the 90's, and they replaced gangster rap for our youth's amusement, as well as youth's culture growth, or lack of growth, depending on our view. The games became fantasy and violent. Our political leaders closed their eyes to what we the people were selling and or buying.

I represented one of the biggest worldwide video game companies. Did music for their movie, as well as TV show. I learned their game and got sick over it. Spoke my mind and acted with my heart and ended up at war with them because the games had no social value but money, teaching what to do when you have fear.

In 2001, I worked on the movie *"Bully"*, which was all about a real-life story of kids in Broward County, FL. These kids killing their bully as they would in a video game. The story is how the group that murdered the bully fell apart when they realized they really killed someone. It was not a game where the dead can come back alive.

Today, video games are "owned" by various militaries around the world. What a great way to see who can become the most desensitized programmed killer. Drones that kill are nothing more than a video game program of live action murder.

By the way, all this clone US killing is done without any constitutional protections of due process. Yep, you the accused do not know the charges. You have not been given a right to defend yourself. Nor be judged by your community. There is only death by a prosecutor who has the power to also be judge and jury, plus executioner. Those who die by accident with the target according to Trump's regime do not count as casualties. No, they are collateral damage.

Mass Democracy Part Two

Democracy was created by mankind, back who knows really when, to do what? What paradigm were the people trying to create?

Democracy to create Justice

Justice?

For who?

Who are we?

What have we become and where are we heading in this Mass Democracy world we all created, and let take our souls to a physical mausoleum of sleep?

Not all of us are asleep. Spiritual insomnia is on the move. The spirits are restless. They are shaking our foundations. Making the earth quake and shake. Throwing storms of tears amid fears that we are behaving out of our agreed boundaries.

Me? I am weathering my storm. I have a mission. This is it. When I am done, I just hope I still can then run and play in this earth I love so much without the shades of shadows our fears and tears have cast on this heaven we created - to live our dreams in physical shape. God willing.

So now, I will continue this indictment of current 21st Century mankind, living in this new prehistoric world. Prehistoric because we do not learn the lessons of our common history to see what is happening now to us.

Extra, Extra, feel all about it. Mass Society moves to Fascism: It's happening. Wake up.

How? You have entered the world of desensitization. A world where we divide each other by political affiliation, color of skin, language you speak, where you were born, sexual preference, just to name a few categories.

See, when division is the game, solutions are not even thought of---let alone talked about. No, we want hate. Hate, and then what?

We want to be better than all the other losers who cannot run our thoughtless lives into the ground of hell here on earth.

For 21st Century fascism to work, you need a political movement catering to the masses who feel left out of society. It's all about following the new leader who has no people program, only a program based on spreading hate and controlling you for the new elite few.

This can only work when we have a new cult of resentment. Because only the few can thrive when material is the end game. To survive, plus thrive, you need a team. Different games, and Mass Democracy is a numbed-down game of life. Perfect for the next inning of history. Both political parties here in America are responsible for this new world. And so are all of us. We know better in our hearts, not just in our minds.

Let's continue with this rise of 21st Century fascism, and then I will give you my thoughts on solutions. It is what I learned from meeting and trying to get people to help my US Senate run, as well as my run for Congress in South Florida. I experienced first-hand the microcosmic world of all cultures living here in the USA.

Mass Democracy is real, based on being politically correct, and doing what the masses do. They all do as they are told, programed to become - what?

Running for political office in the states requires money. From where are you getting your money to represent the people? I learned that it's not from the people unless they get something now. No, you must cater to the powers in control, believing you will sleep with these fleas and change once in office. This is a huge lie.

You become the power's flea. Look at what we are fighting for. People's dignity? No, mass dignity. We are not fighting so our government of the people fulfills its obligation of providing health, welfare and safety to all. We are fighting for the flakes that fall on the floor from the bread WE created for them to control and hold as their own kingdom.

I see this different. I speak so you see and feel what I see and feel. Our representatives work for us, we the people. We need to believe this and live this. This is the secret. You can attract all you wish. But you must live it to have it. Time to change the paradigm.

So, Health, Welfare and Safety. The big three. The purpose of government is to provide for all. You do not just have this as a right. No, your elected officials and their appointed administrative branches, which really run our land, have the duty to provide health, welfare and safety for all. <u>FOR ALL.</u>

So, in our current paradigm, the spiritually-connected intellectuals are put to sleep. The nation becomes a land where those who speak to our nation focus only on material interest. Focus on actively creating resentment. Believing, as Mrs. Clinton calls those who did not like her, "Deplorables."

Gone are the days of the 1960's, where we thought our generation would bring about change. We were then fighting for the cultural and moral improvement of the populace.

The Bernie movement is great as a new beginning, but it does not focus at all on the growth of mankind. It is focused only on how to make a sick patient live in the made-up world of scarcity.

I truly believe;

> "We live in a world of abundance and need to hear the spirit's trumpets begging us to wake up and take back our currency from the Federal Reserve, and Our Government from the puppets of the new elites, the Bankers, who control globalization, saying this is Mass Democracy."

We are up on a tightrope. Our nation is ready to preserve the power of the few to own and control us, by believing their veils of tradition and social order.

We are all witnesses to see ourselves what we have become. Let's take the field and end this insane game.

History teaches us fascism works when society loses its balance. Where there is no middle class. The masses are ready for change and will fall in line behind the "One" who says, I am for you. I will devote my life to the real needs, to the real interest of common man. That is what they usually say. That is what you want to hear. You no longer feel. No, you just blindly believe.

This line between one who works to create a new balance of equal social order, and one who runs to create the darker world of ownership and control, my friends, is very thin.

The Mass Democracy is over, and we the people have a choice; to either fall out of line, or be controlled with these alleged traditional values of the past.

Make our nation great again. By doing what? Recreating a white social order. This is a very bad Rap song. Dark energy.

Or have our nation win the championship of being the land of opportunity for all to live life, have liberty and pursue happiness.

The questions, my friends, are blowing in the wind. Those questions landing on our minds are the following:

Who are we? What do we wish to be?

Another quality of this new leader is they must come from outside the political system, so they can change the system. A true person of the people, who speaks their language, who knows their pain.

Religion becomes very important in this game. The game of Mass religion is really a fascist regime. Today we hate Islamic people, regardless of their intentions. We have a nation that is blaming them for all our ills. What ills? That others will not let the bankers, who run our land, run the common land and people, too. We are a nation owned and controlled by our bankers, the new priests of our era.

Religion is someone's interpretation of God in the past, reduced to words and phrases that share the vision of love that someone else has, and wants you to only feel what they consider to be the eternal truth.

People who did not believe in religion but believed in God, made our nation. They felt, and I agree, that we each need to learn God by living, not repeating chants and slogans only. We need to live in a land that promotes love. A land of God, not under anyone's god, but the God of us all.

We are now running around as if we were a Christian nation doing what other tyrants have done. Kill those who do not agree with our lifestyle.

The Christian Mass religion in various heydays, had many episodes of wrong behavior. Those people who had gained control had apocalyptic visions of and desires for an all-Christian world, ruled by the European whites. Their controlled kingdom of their version of God.

This vision was used by those few who gained control of the masses to have religious wars in the name of God. They burned women at the stake because women did not submit to their interpretation of God. Women have the womb of earth and know the principles of nurturing and caring for the living a lot more than a man who wants to own the world.

These Christians rulers, in their God's name, also separated those who did not belong to their Religion Club and proceeded to kill those others in the name of their God. Remember, Hitler himself was a Jesuit choirboy. And is it not ironic that our current leader is being hailed as chosen by the Christian God to lead, when his entire history is breaking all God's ten commandments. Trump is the set up. He is a jester playing the fool of real evil, trying to make havoc, so they can rule by bringing order to the chaos they helped cause.

Trump is a good man. He is not evil. He is playing a role because he is a narcissist who has been rewarded by society for truly wrong social behavior.

Look at the reason behind the moves. Not the moves. Life is chess and see how we pawns are being played.

People, wake up. Our nation has no vision except borrow and consume. Then, work to pay debt, and go to the doctors and take your pills. *Go ask Alice* as Jefferson Airplane sang, *when she's ten feet tall* are the words I hear now. *Feed your head.* That's right, go to your doctor, get your pills, and numb out your meta/physical self.

We have no trust in politics. We cannot stand our politicians and we allow groups of division to say we need women candidates, instead of, we need candidates who represent all the people. Instead of uniting mankind, these groups are dividing us further.

How do we stop this game? We need a leader of all the people. And this leader cannot be involved in material gain.

<u>Yes, a real leader is involved with gain of the community.</u> Native Indians knew this truth.

Our last Presidential election of 2016 was nothing but an absolute circus. A media carnival that got more people to drop out then drop in. And if you do not vote you deserve what the others vote for you.

There was no content, no message, just hate. We must get involved. Not just the final round, but the whole local and state as well as federal chapter.

People, we need to answer the basic question of every civilization throughout time. That question is:

"What is a just society?"

Not be sold the answer, but we must feel it. A society based on fear mongering and the resulting hate is the wrong society. The delusion that the enemy is coming to kill us, must stop.

Trump gains office by disrespecting woman as a gender, people by nationality different than his and his family's backgrounds, and by religion, too. But he is not alone, and we get off on watching this insane behavior.

Trump is a leader of which people? Remember, he did not win the popular vote of the 45 percent of the 100 percent of people who could have voted and chose not to vote.

Mrs. Clinton was worse, in my mind. Why? Because you know what Trump is, so deal with it. Clinton? Who is she?

This woman manipulates, lies and speaks one way but walks and acts in the exact opposite way. But she controlled the "liberal" media. So, we are sold a different Clinton. She poses as if she is a noun. Not a living thing.

As Karl Rove, the creator of Bush the Second himself told me back in 1999:

> "The game is to cater to those who actually vote. To bring in other voters would change the game that politicians and those who control the politician's play".

Let us recap.

What is Mass Democracy?

One, it is a society where the media is owned by the party who runs your nation. The party who runs our nation is the independent third-party banking system we call the Federal Reserve. Yes, understand this truth. Stop believing the Fed reports to our government. Please wake up.

To stay in power, they must control our thought patterns. This they do by stimulating us today with what everyone can have if you, the individual, behave and follow the golden rules of those few who slip through the system, and become celebrities.

When intellectuals try to speak, they are not given a mass media pulpit. They are removed from the mass public.

When an outsider runs for office, that outsider is not able to get any notice because the outsider needs money to show that the outsider is a real candidate.

The exception is a person who has money, and gets mass media. This person will run as an outsider and attract voters by claiming to be the one that will help those that the system ignores. But in truth, that outsider can be just one running to join the system, or one running to make the new paradigm.

I ran to change the system.

As a candidate for Congress this year, I believed in gun control. But I ran as a democrat, with a good chance to join the party as their candidate.

Game ended when they tried to control my words. I was given a sheet from the Democratic party telling me what not to say regarding gun control. And then they told me what to say.

Examples being the following:

- Stay away from Gun Control. Say Prevent gun violence.
- Stay away from stricter gun laws. Say common sense reforms.
- Stay away from gun owners/supports. Do not say NRA lobbyists and gun manufacturers.
- Stay away from mental illness or criminals. Say people with dangerous histories.
- Stay away from gun rights. Say responsible gun ownership.
- Stay away from laws or policies. Say safety or security.
- Stay away from mass shootings. Say saving our children's lives.

This is Mass Democracy at work. Let's be politically correct. We need not offend the people who profit off our Mass Democracy. Heck, we will even socialize their losses and privatize their gains. All in the Mass Democracy name of elite stupidity. Too big to fail, we are told. So big that the puppets are scared to prosecute those few for theft and fraud. SAD.

Not only did I not follow their lead, I also offered more solutions. Like control the sale of bullets. Put markers on bullets so we know who sold and who bought those bullets. And, stop giving kids drugs to control their moods. Teach them how to live their moods. Mankind used to do just that before our few controllers figured out how to make us a society of zombies. All so those vampires could feed off the rest.

Education in Mass democracy is where it all begins. The brainwashing of our young. To fall in line and not question, just be part of the system. There is no character formation in Mass Democracy. Nope. All you learn is how to grab a ring on this economic society of unequal. What you are taught is the only system. Another lie. And you even borrow monies so you stay forever in this fake debt.

In the world of Mass Democracy education there is no absolute eternal truths. Because if it is eternal, one must be prepared for changes which never end. But in Mass Democracy, you are taught man can conquer all. A lie.

No, you are taught that earning money is all that is important in life. Ask around, see what the happiness factor is in our land called the USA. Not very high. Not everyone can succeed in this money game. Most will fail, and hate will surface, and that hate will take control of your minds. Which allows for the few to take control. In this era, Trump did not figure this game out. No, he figured out how he could get control and used our mass media, because his acts gave the media the audience they needed to sell and sell what the advertisers wanted to sell to we the people.

We the people, by our actions and non-actions allow our nation to be taken by a new form of televised division and hate. Trump will not be the final leader. The mess he creates will either free us or incarcerate our land for many generations to come. The answer will appear. We need to attract the energy we wish to live.

If we do not go back to a moral education, the naked truth is the following:

- Violence will not be banished.
- More laws or stronger punishments will not end the violence.
- More pills will be sold to numb the general population out even more.

Only the development of conscience will lead the way back to a higher civilization. This is the betrayal of the elites. They set the stage to protect their lofty position in public life. To them, only maintaining their power matters.

And to do so, you must remove reason from our consciousness. Sooner or later the bottom will fall out and fascism will return stronger than before.

Fascism is a seed that we need to permanently extinguish, and to do so means have a just society for all. The democracy our founding fathers tried to create.

It is a big game and no one player is in control. It is a team game, and many do not realize they are actually doing what they are doing.

Only a true outsider of the scarcity this system creates can see the illusion of these man-made rules and regulations. I see them as the imaginary prisons of mind control of the masses in picture terms - the forest created by the trees in their game board of controlling life.

But the game is even worse. This is the quarterback sneak for the winning touchdown at the current goal line. Dark vs. light. The evil that we let run our earth's 21st Century currency.

The play?

The One World Order

The IMF & Industrial War Machines Game Plan

The One World Order

Now to the new crime of mankind. We are militarizing our police. This is the game and this is fascism. Again.

The end game of Mass Democracy is a world of national fascism.

Mass Democracy divides us into two sides. But unites us when an enemy is identified that must be eliminated or contained.

Mass Media is today corporately-owned or controlled by the WASP- controlled banking system. Run by, and for this banking crew, who have bankrupted our culture of independent thoughts to build new communities dreams. Mass media today stops the building of teams.

If you do not agree, you are labeled an outsider.

The game of mass media is to perpetuate the hegemonic society rules of the land, sea and air. In all aspects of life.

We have surveillance controls that monitor everything. Every breath you take. Every announced thought you have.

The goal of this banking elite is simple to follow. Let's learn the three goals to own and control our time here on earth. Then look at your lives.

First goal is to keep the people of the announced industrial first world in this hegemonic ruling order in line. To make sure we obey. Who are these nations? The nations of the EU, USA, Canada, Australia, Japan and Russia.

The wild card is Russia. A nation so big it has 11 time zones. With a very small population, the nation could go astray. That is why we have a mixed media when we hear about Russia.

We, the first world order, recently gave the World Cup and the Olympics to Russia. Sports that showcase the First World Banking order of commerce and trade. Hope is to keep the people in line.

Russia could join the nations of Group Two. Make a new world order. And this could happen without China joining this second world order. As China is the real enemy of the WASP ruling society.

So how do we keep the first world societies in line? Make fear and spread random death? Then create a new army of thought controls by domestic security and police being militarized. Make the people scared of each other. Keep dividing us by keeping resources of necessities private.

Then have the cure. Blame others for your needs. Get the scapegoats, Immigrants, Muslims, Blacks, Mexicans, Gays, etc. Then build walls on borders. Make us hate one another.

Goal Two is to get the second world nations to join this Banking club way of life.

The second world, according to this crew, are the following nations: Mexico, Brazil, China, India, South Africa and maybe, Iran. Goal here is to get these few to be in our system, which we know as the IMF bankers.

China and Iran are problems. China is its own civilization. Does not need our world controls. Iran is a wildcard. Could join China or us.

Trade does keep China, the nation, engaged. But know that China is the oldest living society on earth, and will never submit.

Group three are everyone else. Game here is keep these land and water-rich societies in line. Make them use our first world banking system.

Make these nations submit to our economic world by destroying all opposition to thoughts different than our controlling order. Just see what we do to those who do not submit. Look around. North Korea, Iran and Cuba, to name but three. China is too big to attack, so we try to cut them off at the head. Make sure no one joins their banking system.

Use our corporate culture to be the virtues of living in this new world, better order. Make everyone want to be American. The land that sells you McDonalds and Coca Cola, and bankrolls Monsanto.

Goal Three is to find rulers who will submit to your rule. Make them part of your club. Then stage fake elections in these lands.

Britain, in its top dog day, created kings, and then made those kings the rulers of their lands, and part of the alleged British commonwealth. That is what the UK did to these group two and three nations. Remember, Britain made its Empire selling people, selling drugs and stealing resources. Then selling those resources back to the land in their new shape. Example: cotton, now as clothes.

After World War One, outside of Iran and Egypt, the UK carved the lands of the Ottoman Turk Empire into Kingdoms that submitted to UK rule. Exceptions being Israel and Lebanon.

But Israel, being displaced Jews from Central Europe, was the perfect front to have a first world state in that landmass called the Middle East. These Jews believe God chose them. That rallying cry is how they survived the Vatican in the Dark Ages, making them the scapegoat of the Vatican's' hegemonic European control.

Israel today is the second home of the military-industrial machine that secures this first world way of life. They had to in order to survive the third world Palestinians. An enemy for no reason but division.

Israel makes and sells the machines that spy and kill the people who disagree with this banking order. Big profit, too. They also are the home to technology to feed the people of the world. And not the Monsanto way.

This game of division in Israel will end because the people are tired of hating each other for no consciousness reason. Hate to protect an independent banking order is really screwed up. Not God's idea. I will do all I can to help bring this about.

When I went to Jerusalem this spring, I saw the American shopping style mall on the Tower of David entry point. I could not believe the gentrification of this holy city to three religions.

The Palestinians are caged in what is called the West Bank and Gaza. They can be released, I guess, when they submit to this way of first world banker's order. Or when the people say no more. And I believe we should get the terrorists in exchange. More on this in another time. I see how to mend their broken hearts.

Let me now move to the third world nation we call Cuba. Cuba, a land I love. This land, regardless of Castro's crimes, and yes, he killed, with no moral authority, is made up of people today who do not put material before each other.

The government of this land will change. Castro, the brother, will die. There is no successor with the karma and charisma to carry through a one man-controlled society. Cuba will open up and the trick is to keep it pure as it becomes a 21st century nation. I hope and pray they do not kill their neighborhood high morals.

Art and sport rule this land. Education is their key. No killing gangs. A land where people root for each other.

Yes, it has its problems. And the big one is the US. We have absolute moral-deficient clowns like Marco

Rubio, whom I ran against for the Senate, trying to punish Cuba - for whom and who?

Not feeding people, sharing our excess without making them just like us, is absolute human abuse. And a violation of all-natural universal truths. The Cubans reject our olive branch because than the media will say, see they need America. We all need each other, and sooner or later, the embargo will not justify the absence of living standards the Cubans endure for Castro themes to continue to control the land and its people.

Look at Rubio for a moment. Nothing between his ears that was not put there by the controllers who said do as we say, and we will provide. Rubio is just one of many on both sides of the US political parties' playing field. Absolutely doing as they are told.

Rubio being one of many and just my example, is controlled by those who caused the cold war. The war that made America the industrial military machine we have become. Rubio's puppet masters need an enemy, so let's keep the Cubans on that team. If the US had embraced Castro in 1960, instead of pushing him to Russia, history would be different. Again, know the game; we need an enemy.

Remember, Castro replaced a US-placed monster, Batista. The first flood of Cuban refugees were many well-heeled members of this Batista absolute dictatorship rule. A rule that allowed US companies to have Cuba as their paradise of mafia-run entertainment venues that was justified because the United States was God's chosen nation, without ever informing you. Whose God?

And these few immigrants were given the ability to create Cuba II. A Cuban mafia, living in southern Florida, making a mess so they can get Cuba back and allow the IMF to steal resources, saying capitalism is the only way. Capitalism, the system that robs you of your resources, is the game these few people play. Then make those resources scarce, so the few own and control you.

Let's end this lie.

Or do you like being comfortable numb?

Do you like an empty head?

Do you like doing what you told?

Mass Democracy Part Three

The Totalitarian World Order.

Or, the return to heaven, here on earth.

How do we safeguard our consciousness?

Truth: The just government must appear. How?

By creating the 21st Century government that follows the eternal truths of why a government should exist.

These truths are to insure the people the life, liberty and pursuit of happiness - that was promised when our land was created back in 1776. The principles have not changed, but our understanding of eternal truths has. Our statesmen must be willing to have nothing, and then be the real leader of our group, a band of 21st century men.

Here is what I believe we need to do to reset our land.

At this moment, technology has taken over our land. It controls who we are and what we do, what we think, and gets us to feel what others want us to feel. It must stop. It is our mind's mood pill. And it allows others to sell us their pills of thought control and physical control

Let's start with the big four. Apple, Amazon, Google and Facebook. These companies need to be run by <u>the governments of the people,</u> and not by the elites running the government. These companies are really data collectors.

The small networks of individuals that were created when these organizations were babies are now part of a vacuum-cleaning beast that mines data and sells the data for profit.

They are too big to be owned by the few for their profit. They have become the machine of technology that owns and controls our minds and shuts down our souls.

The kids that created Facebook actually allowed the few to create apps on top of their social network platform. Their platform stores data. The wants and needs of you--the public as you share or moan to others what you want and need when you awake, get bored during the day or before you shut down and go to sleep. MIND CONTROL.

Trump's campaign used a company based in the UK called Cambridge Analytica to mine the data, and then go through the computer-stored "gold dust" it found. It used this gold dust to make the info fit into different shapes and sizes by asking the data to go into different groups that answered certain questions, all to determine how to make our Facebook users angry enough about their lives and do something like vote for the alleged outsider called Trump. Or not vote for Clinton. Or just stay numb and drop out of the election.

Again, the data was mined to make the data give the insights to the heart and souls of the people whose data Facebook allowed the Company to mine for a fee. A fee, so it could show the public the system works and brings in money, not limited to anyone or any purpose but makes money and the stock price should go up. We are all part of this insane game of money first and foremost.

I must add an important truth right now. <u>Trump and his entire empire are not outsiders. No, they are part of the money-first game.</u> He chose the Republican Party for his values, where the good old white WASP days were about to become history. Going, going, and then long gone. He read the tea leaves. The Democratic Party has no theme, only more of the same. Trump ran as an angry Republican.

Both parties have the same bank control. Same handouts. Same we will give you this if we get power.

But the truth is they have a duty to provide the health, welfare and safety for our entire community of equals. This is a duty, for we all deserve living in this time period, not just the ones that made these few educated brainwashing elites.

The Democratic Party of the Clinton's is done. The youth will inherit the world and this thought process must be buried, as it is a relic of dinosaurs' mind control. When information was withheld, and truth was a secret.

So, time for a third party to appear, as the Republicans did in 1856. That party freed the slaves and changed our government. Today's party is on the road to fascism. Needs to stop.

Trump is in control. Trump sold himself as an outsider to the public because he was an outsider to the puppet game of politicians and bought campaigns. But he was no outsider to Mass Democracy. He was one of the leaders who sold himself as the shock voice of entrepreneurs. But I must add, entrepreneurs with no moral values in our current times. And TV-needing viewers to sell to advertisers, to buy ads loved his routine.

Now how do we return to a land of moral values? One where we create a path for all to pursue happiness?

We give each other a government that has a duty to provide the health welfare and safety to all its citizens, regardless of social rank or gender, race, sexual preference, religious preference or any man-made class distinction.

This is a minimum. Let's call it a coach ticket to a living standard for all. The lack of this simple truth creates the fear of uncertainty and allows the few to control the all.

Then we change the election rules of our nation. What we do is put a limit on what you can spend and when you can spend it. No more begging and selling your souls for cash. No. You run for office at the same starting gate. We stop the ads on the public airwaves. This change is a game changer. The ads for the public using the public airwaves must not be for private profit, which perpetuates the insanity of Mass Democracy.

Education must be public and for all. If you want private school, pay for it. But the public must have an option to be educated by our government. And yes, we can afford it. If I ruled the thoughts, I would have college fees free in public universities, providing the student pays back society for half the time they went to school on the public, by doing community service before private business as a full-time job. After hours, go create but working hours, you must give back to society what they gave you. And society will pay you a living wage.

And school must teach the humanities. We must share our creating knowledge of fellow mankind as we discover our living space here on earth and inside our universe. We must teach you to create. And know it is not abnormal. We all have the ability to do it if you try. We must return to love of all, not hate for anyone not just like me.

Saying that, we must create jobs financed by the various governments to provide all community occupations. From teachers, to street cleaners, to police and firemen, and nurses during after school hours of the arts and crafts, as well as sports. We must have local communities support the people. And the people must support the local communities. That is how a heart works. It gives and takes. So must we in our daily living routines.

Politicians must stop saying elect me, I will be bringing jobs back. They are gone, and this is a different period in the history of our human race. We need to create new jobs and opportunities for this era. Stop living the past. Leave the dirt of time alone. We can do it. We are the currency. We are abundance, not scarcity.

People need people. We must learn how to all get along. Why can't we all be friends? We can, if everyone has equal opportunities.

We must provide as a minimum, health care for all citizens. A single pay system. And this health care is more than just fix with pills what is damaged or broken inside our bodies. This health care includes teaching you about what you need to do to stay healthy.
Make you aware of what you put into your body or what we, society put into your body.

Which brings me to the role of a government. Government's role is to stop wrong behavior of the few who harm the rest. Especially when circumstances change, and we learn what we accepted before has consequences we were not aware of then, and now understand. I am talking about the food we eat, the water we drink, and the air we breathe.

Now let's finish what we must do to create our just society, in line with our promise to God. The promise that our nation would provide life, liberty, and the pursuit of happiness to all its living people.

We must stop chemicals in our foods and elsewhere. This is a must. Our bodies were not made to digest these creations of man. Our bodies run on living nature. Nature with the essence called life. Chemicals have no life force. They kill the machines that mother nature and God created for us to live in and enjoy physical life.

The chemicals we put on our lawns to keep them artificially green must end. We need to stop putting chemicals in the water as well as in the air.

Anything that goes up does come down. Gravity is this rule. These chemicals in the air or land and seas kill.

And they kill slowly which may be good for pharmaceutical companies' paper profits but does nothing for society as a whole. Plus, there is the boomerang effect where this will harm the families and friends of those who commit these man-made crimes.

And I must add, wrong behavior by a corporation is wrong behavior by the individuals that caused and did the act. There must be personal liability both civil and criminal.

The environment of our lives must be protected if we really want health care for all. We need to stop fossil fuels of all kinds being how we run our society. There is a reason earth buried the gases and black gold called oil under the ground. The spiritual reason this occurred was because it does not serve the living in any way.

I wish to bring this book to its conclusion. This book is to hear the spirit behind the winds, the rain, and the fires of our world. We need to live with earth, and with God.

We are today the fallen race of mankind. We are all about the selfie. Even Apple, and its phones of control, promote taking selfie pictures to share how great we are.

I, too, am guilty of me before we. But I am aware, and this book is the indictment of me and all of us that believe we are living the life. But whose life? Not ours.

We are a nation created to share as a team our community. We started out so strong only to surrender. We are the fallen. We have surrendered to mammon. The man created and promoted desire for possessions. The marketing process of Big Time is really the process of us hiding from our souls.

We need to give everyone a jubilee from all debts. We need to start again. We need to end slave interest. Immediately.

The bible we worship, in Deuteronomy section 15.1, says that after seven years of debt, you who own the debt must cancel the debt. Give the debtor the opportunity to win again. Then let the debtor's consciousness decide what to do for you. Remember the song, *That's Life. High in April and broke in May? But back on top in June.* We all have our swoons, so let's let everyone win. And if your debt is cancelled, deduct it from your taxes. We need to give everyone a chance, like the bible says.

We need everyone to believe. We need to live this year, not last year. We need to all win. We need entrepreneurs to breathe again. We need capitalism dispossession to end.

Let the morally correct version of investment to rise from the shadows of our sick islander desires. No society is an island and we need to all bring back the human race.

America, our Columba, where are you now? Don't you care about your sons and daughters?

And saying that, let's make it worldwide. People, don't you care about your sons and daughters? Let's become Abrahams' children. Before your descendants change the game.

There is one God, and we need to choose GOD. One first creation of physical existence and mental thought conditions. Yes, we need to choose God and live with our catcher, who tells us where to pitch and what to pitch. Make it God's game.

My friends, that is the Columba. That is our eternity if we can do it here on earth. We can. Pray, and see and do. Do not just pray. Visualize, and make it happen. You can, if we all close our eyes together and see where we all come from.

To some, this is the end. To others, this is a new beginning, my friends. We need a new beginning of our choosing as a group living with God. Not under god, but with God.

This is my spiritual insomnia. Trying to make a fairy tale of our consciousness come true. Trying to make the heaven we dream **of a living reality.**

Remember, *fairy tales can come true when you're young at heart.* That line is from a song my mom used to sing to me.

Mom, who was a great card player, knew the truth, just did not live it, in the end. She gave me those words of wisdom then, and said, "Stevie, live life this way and all your dreams can and will come true."

Mom I pray you're right. I will do my role to make you right.

I will never give up.

And Dad, as we discussed, do not give choice, share reason.

This book is dedicated to all of you.

May we finally wake up.

www.ingramcontent.com/pod-product-compliance
Lightning Source LLC
LaVergne TN
LVHW021701060526
838200LV00050B/2456